personal struggles which soon embroiled the state.

Few Virginians anticipated that massive resistance would actually result in laws that would close the doors of public schools, but this happened in Norfolk, Warren County, and Charlottesville. When hastily established private schools proved an unsatisfactory substitute, public opinion began to call for reopening public schools.

In January, 1959, the Virginia Supreme Court of Appeals handed down the decision which nullified the massive resistance laws and led Governor Almond and other state officials to concede. "The truth came quietly home to many Southern politicians that 'you can't win' against the Supreme Court and the government of the United States."

Virginia's maneuvers may well serve as a test case for other states in the Old South still faced with the complex problem of eventual school desegregation. What happened in her struggle has sharpened the alternatives, for, as Mr. Muse concludes, "It resolved the issue pragmatically into one of desegregation as ordered by federal courts or the closing of schools. The dreadful alternative of abandoning public education is now the single desperate road of defiance. In the last analysis even the Deep South will not go down that road."

VIRGINIA'S MASSIVE RESISTANCE

VIRGINIA'S MASSIVE RESISTANCE

by Benjamin Muse

INDIANA UNIVERSITY PRESS

Bloomington

Part of the material in chapter 7 is adapted from an article
by the author in The New Republic *of September 17, 1956*

TO BEATRIZ
my partner in all things

CONTENTS

1. INITIAL REACTION

VIRGINIA in the middle of the twentieth century was in some ways more a Northern than a Southern state. Its economy faced the North. Businessmen shuttled constantly back and forth between Richmond and Norfolk and New York. Few Virginians found reason to travel in the Deep South. Hardly a Virginia town was without its subscribers to the *New York Times;* the *Atlanta Constitution* was rarely seen in this state.

Looking at the Old Dominion in the spring of 1954, one would have found little to suggest an attitude of strident hostility to a Supreme Court decision against race segregation in the public schools. On the contrary, there were a number of reasons for expecting that Virginia would lead the states of the Old South in adjustment to the high court's ruling.

A period of recalcitrance was indeed to be expected in one quarter. There was one section where Negroes were as numerous in proportion to whites as in the Black Belts of Alabama and Mississippi. In thirty counties in southern and eastern Virginia Negroes were over 40 per cent of the total population. In this area race prejudice was deeply rooted; any change in the traditional pattern of segregation was regarded here as too impossible to be seriously discussed. This section was not typical of the state as a whole; and all the people residing in these thirty counties, both white and colored, represented less than 15 per cent of the inhabitants of Virginia. It is of ominous significance, nevertheless, that this section throughout Virginia history, and still in 1954, wielded political power vastly out of proportion to its population.

In all Virginia, the ratio of Negroes to the total population had declined by 1950 to 22.2 per cent, a figure only a little higher than that in Maryland (where the official policy was to be one of loyal compliance with the Supreme Court ruling). In half of Virginia Negroes were no more common than in many sections of the North. In twenty-one counties and three cities Negro residents ranged from none at all to 5 per cent of the total population.

Many, assuming a cheerful acceptance of subordinate status on the part of the Negroes, were unaware of any race problem in this state. Governor John S. Battle, who was in office from 1950 to 1954, later said to a federal court with obvious sincerity: "I think there were no serious problems as far as the races are concerned before 1954."

Interracial relations were, indeed, relatively good in Virginia. V. O. Key, Jr. had written in 1949, in *Southern Politics:* "Virginia's white citizens in and out of the machine have demonstrated a relatively acute sense of responsibility toward the Negro—an attitude that may account in part for the fact that its race relations are perhaps the most harmonious in the South."

A Negro had been elected to the Richmond city council in 1949. Negroes served on the school boards of a number of Virginia cities and on the governing boards of several counties.

The desegregation of state institutions of higher learning had proceeded entirely without incident. The University of Virginia had begun accepting a few Negro students in 1950, the Medical College of Virginia and the Richmond Professional Institute in 1951, and the Virginia Polytechnic Institute in 1953. A few days before the Supreme Court decision of 1954, the Catholic Bishop of Richmond had announced that Catholic parochial schools would be desegregated the following September; and sixty Negro pupils were integrated then among 5,228 white pupils in fourteen parochial schools.

Negroes who were qualified with respect to the poll tax requirement voted without difficulty in Virginia. The poll tax contributed to Virginia's dubious distinction of ranking near the bottom of the list of states in the percentage of population participating in elections, but it applied to whites and Negroes alike. In some of the counties of heavy Negro population, timidity and a fear of risking white displeasure kept all but a relative handful of colored citizens from the polls; but there were almost no overt attempts to keep Negroes from registering and voting in this state. Officials of the National Association for the Advancement of Colored People stated publicly that they had no complaint on this score.

Something approaching physical equality had at last been achieved in public provision for the education of white and Negro children. The salaries of white and Negro public school teachers had been brought to an exactly equal scale. Negro pupils represented approximately 24 per cent of the total school population; Negro schools accounted for approximately 21 per cent of the total valuation of public school property in Virginia.

During three years of litigation in the school cases, in which a Virginia school board was one of the original defendants, the Old Dominion had awaited the outcome with anxiety, but with traditional respect for the Supreme Court of the United States. In March, 1954, by way of preparing for the coming Supreme Court decision, the executive committee of the Virginia Council of Churches had issued a statement saying:

We recognize the tardiness of the Christian community in forthrightly dealing with this problem. . . . We urge prayerful and serious study of it in the spirit of boundless, courageous, intelligent good will—which is the spirit of Jesus Christ. When the Supreme Court of the United States shall have expressed itself on the matter, we call upon our brothers to receive its expression peacefully and in good faith.

Shortly before the Supreme Court decision was delivered, I had a long talk with Dowell J. Howard, the State Superintendent of Public Instruction. This earnest and capable official regarded it as a foregone conclusion that the Court would rule against segregation, and it did not seem to have occurred to him that Virginia would do other than address itself to the hard task of compliance. He had already wrestled quietly with the problem for a long time. He was grimly confident that gradual adjustment could be accomplished in two-thirds of Virginia; with regard to the other one-third he could only say that it would take a long time. I sensed in him a certain exhilaration at the prospect of becoming, himself, a central figure in great events, and pride in the thought that Dowell Howard might be destined to lead Virginia's public school system through the greatest crisis in its history.

(Eighteen months later Howard suffered a nervous breakdown, and he died in February, 1956, of a heart attack.)

When, on May 17, 1954, the Supreme Court handed down its momentous decision, Howard said to the press: "There will be no defiance of the Supreme Court as far as I am concerned. We are trying to teach children to abide by the law of the land, and we will abide by it."

Many leaders expressed regret and deep concern, but the initial reaction to the Supreme Court decision in Richmond was loyal and constructive. State Attorney General J. Lindsay Almond, Jr., who had argued the case for school segregation before that Court, said now: "The highest court in the land has spoken and I trust that Virginia will approach the question realistically and endeavor to work out some rational adjustment."

The *Richmond News Leader* called for the formulation of "a proposal that would win the Supreme Court's approval," and suggested: "If the court were to fix, say a ten-year period, and permit the states to integrate 10 per cent of their schools a year . . . a solution might be found."

Governor Thomas Bahnson Stanley said, in a statement issued a few hours after the Supreme Court decision was announced:

I contemplate no precipitate action, but I shall call together as quickly as practicable representatives of both state and local governments to consider the matter and work toward a plan which will be acceptable to our citizens and in keeping with the edict of the court.

In Washington, Virginia's Senator Harry F. Byrd issued a sharply critical statement. Byrd called the decision "the most serious blow that has been struck against the rights of the states," and said Virginia faced "a crisis of the first magnitude." His language was not inflammatory. "Whatever is done," he said, "should be based on our most mature judgment after sober and exhaustive consideration." But significantly, Byrd gave no hint of acceptance of the ruling, no suggestion of compromise.

2. THE BEGINNINGS OF DEFIANCE

No AREA of the state outside of the successive capital cities of
Jamestown, Williamsburg and Richmond has seen more of history than the Fourth Congressional District in southeastern
Virginia. In the last stages of the War Between the States this
area witnessed the devastation of the long siege of Petersburg
and Lee's surrender at Appomattox.

The Fourth District is the core of the area of heavy Negro
population. It is sometimes called the Black Belt, but is more
often referred to nowadays merely as Southside Virginia.
Changing by a county or two with periodical redistricting, the
Fourth District has remained the area of greatest concentration
of Negro population since colonial times. In 1890 Negroes represented 65 per cent of the district's residents. Backward economically, the Fourth has been almost stationary in population
growth for half a century. Its population, according to the
census of 1950, was 171,211 whites and 167,139 non-whites.

Nevertheless, the influence of the Fourth District and
Southside Virginia upon state policy is great, especially when
a problem of race is involved. It is enhanced by the circumstance that the capital city itself lies close to this area. Southside Virginia sends a disproportionate number of representatives to state meetings of various kinds in Richmond. Southside
leaders are easy and frequent callers at the offices of the governor and other state officials. In contrast, a visit to Richmond
for representatives of northern and western Virginia, where
Negroes are few and race prejudice is at a minimum, even today is a serious undertaking. It may involve over 300 miles of
travel each way.

The race problem has plagued the Fourth as no other district. In 1831 the area was the scene of Nat Turner's terrifying slave insurrection. In the years immediately following the War Between the States, the Fourth District was the chief center of Negro political power. In 1888 it elected Representative John W. Langston, the only Negro ever to represent Virginia in Congress.

Prince Edward County, whose school board was one of the original defendants in the litigation leading to the Supreme Court decision of May 17, 1954, is in Virginia's Fourth District.

On June 20, 1954, a group of Fourth District leaders met in the Petersburg fire house and declared themselves "unalterably opposed" to racial integration in the schools. The District's Congressman, Watkins M. Abbitt, and sixteen of its eighteen representatives in the state legislature attended this meeting, over which State Senator Garland Gray presided. During the same week, huge delegations of Fourth District citizens descended upon the Governor's office with a similar message. The Petersburg fire-house group also circularized the governing boards of all Virginia counties; and, in the weeks following, sixty-one of them responded by adopting resolutions urging the continuance of segregated schools.

During the same period the very many white Virginians who accepted the inevitability of school desegregation found no occasion to speak out, or to visit the Governor. They appeared to expect that, with some localized resistance, the matter would slowly work itself out.

On June 25, executing a sharp change from his moderate statement five weeks earlier, Governor Stanley declared: "I shall use every legal means at my command to continue segregated schools in Virginia."

The Governor's new statement gave administration encouragement to the movement of resistance rising in Southside

Virginia and soon to spread over half the state. Coming from a particularly docile disciple of Senator Byrd, it was quickly recognized also as the Byrd policy, and the line to be followed by Byrd's famous political organization in all sections. From then on, denunciation of the Supreme Court and defiance of its edict were the approved procedure for all ambitious followers of the Senator.

Certainly a great deal of hostility to the Supreme Court ruling was spontaneous, and many politicians followed a natural impulse in voicing their resentment. The vast majority of white Virginians undoubtedly preferred segregated schools. But, if it had been ordained by the leader of Virginia's dominant political organization, a policy of reluctant acceptance of the law of the land and a gradual adjustment to it would have been by no means impossible.

As it happened, a dynamic and contagious grass-roots force joined with a power at the political summit in a combination which moderate elements in Virginia were unable effectively to resist for four turbulent years.

In September Governor Stanley set up a commission to study the problem posed by the Supreme Court decision and submit appropriate recommendations. Having as its chairman State Senator Gray (who had presided over the Petersburg firehouse meeting), it became known as the Gray Commission, and its recommendations, which were to come forth fourteen months later, were called the Gray Plan. Gray was a wealthy Fourth District leader and prominent Byrd organization politician, who was often mentioned as a possible candidate for governor.

On October 8, 1954, a significant meeting was held in the town of Blackstone in the heart of the Fourth District. Prominent citizens from all sections of the district gathered there and formed an organization to insist on a continuance of public school segregation. There was no thought of reviving the Ku Klux Klan; that organization was completely discredited in Virginia. With an instinctive feeling of Virginia superiority, the White Citizens Councils, which were springing up elsewhere in the South, were also eschewed. These Fourth District leaders gave their organization the resounding name of "Defenders of State Sovereignty and Individual Liberties."

A number of other segregationist organizations were later to appear on the Virginia scene. Some would dissolve after a few months; others would survive, with modest membership. The list includes the National Protective Individual Rights, Inc., the Virginia League, the Crusaders for Constitutional Government, the Seaboard White Citizens Council and several plain White Citizens Councils. In spite of occasional missionary forays from North Carolina, the Ku Klux Klan never gained a foothold in this state. The Defenders of State Sovereignty and Individual Liberties was to become by far the largest organization of pro-segregation extremists in Virginia. It was to become also a powerful political force.

After a second meeting, the Defenders issued a statement proposing a constitutional revision to permit the public school system to be abolished; at the same time it announced the appointment of William F. Moxey, Jr. as full-time secretary. Moxey resigned as commissioner of revenue of Powhatan County to accept the post. Collins Denny, a well-known Richmond attorney, was employed as counsel. An able speaker, of distinguished presence, Denny was to represent the Defenders on many public occasions. Robert B. Crawford, of Farmville, in Prince Edward County, was chosen permanent Defenders president.

Crawford was typical of many previously little-known individuals who have come into prominence and no little power in the South by leading movements of extreme segregationists. A man of integrity, and as it developed, of considerable ability, Crawford impressed many with the sincerity of his segregationist views. He was a Farmville dry-cleaner and had served fifteen years on the Prince Edward County school board. He was to become a frequent consultant of the Governor and other state leaders and a major influence in state affairs.

At the time of the issuance of their charter on October 26, 1954, the Defenders' membership numbered 2,000 in thirteen chapters, most of them in the Fourth District. The organization was to grow to a membership of about 8,000 by November, 1955, and about 12,000 by the end of 1956, with chapters scattered widely over the state. Its members were regarded as the spokesmen for a much larger number of extreme segregationists.

The organization's charter declared its objective to be the defense of state rights "by all honorable and lawful means." The Defenders of State Sovereignty, although aggressive and uncompromising, was more decorous in its methods and less given to reckless bluster than most segregationist organizations. If, indeed, its small and noisy unit in Arlington County resembled a White Citizens Council in the Deep South, elsewhere its activities were generally in keeping with the traditionally genteel tone of Virginia politics. It was eminently respectable; politicians were happy to speak at Defenders rallies and to share the platform with Defenders speakers on other occasions.

3. PRINCE EDWARD COUNTY

INITIAL resistance to the Supreme Court's school desegregation order in Virginia, and in the South, was undoubtedly encouraged by the fact that the only strictly Southern localities involved in the original litigation were two rural Black Belt counties in which any degree of racial integration would be most difficult to bring about.

Had the revolutionary social change been initiated in one, or two, of a hundred Southern counties on the Appalachian plateau, where Negroes represent only a small fraction of the total population, it would have moved faster and with less convulsion than has been the case. If the original decree could have named merely some of these relatively easy localities, Southerners might have conceived of a gradual process which would reach the Black Belt only in its later stages. But, viewing the Supreme Court decree first in terms of immediate integration in Clarendon County, South Carolina, and Prince Edward County, Virginia, it was not unnatural for many to say: "Compliance is impossible." In actual fact, at this writing, in the fall of 1960, no move toward school integration has yet been made in either of those two counties.

In the Summerton school district, out of which the Clarendon County case arose, there were 2,799 Negro children and only 295 white children. Robert McC. Figg, of Charleston, one of the attorneys for the Summerton school board, thought the seeming impossibility of desegregation there made it fortunate for the segregationist cause that the Summerton case had come to the Supreme Court. "We'd be fools to destroy this case," he said. "This case is a hammer!"

The National Association for the Advancement of Colored

People probably thought that the Clarendon County case was a hammer too. Implementation of the Supreme Court ruling was not attempted in that county, beyond a no-time-limit district court order, secured in July, 1955, for desegregation "with all deliberate speed," until a new suit was filed in April, 1960.

But the original suit against the school board of Prince Edward County was pressed relentlessly through a series of hearings, decisions, appeals, re-hearings, decisions, appeals, etc. until a final desegregation order resulted in the abandonment of public education in that county.

Negroes represented 71 per cent of the total population in Clarendon County. In Prince Edward Negroes were only 45 per cent of the total. However, they accounted for approximately 53 per cent of the public school enrollment, and Prince Edward lies in the heart of that section of Virginia, described in the preceding chapter, where abandonment of segregation was nearest to inconceivable. (Incidentally, Prince Edward adjoins another county of fateful memory—Appomattox.) The school litigation in Prince Edward arose in 1951, not out of discontent with segregation, but out of a desire for a new Negro high school. It became a desegregation suit only when NAACP attorneys declined to lend their services in a suit based on the separate-but-equal doctrine. A new high school had already been built, at the cost of approximately $850,000, when the Supreme Court decision was handed down. Few less propitious places could have been found outside of the Deep South in which to attempt the first adjustment to the new order in interracial relations.

During the year following the decision of May 17, 1954, most of the white people of Prince Edward went about their business with mingled feelings of anxiety, disbelief, and fatuous hope. The people of this Virginia county are little given to public demonstrations; desegregation of their schools was simply regarded by the white community as something that could not happen. By a melancholy coincidence the Supreme Court decree of May 31, 1955, was handed down on the last day under Virginia law for the adoption of the county's annual budget. The governing body of Prince Edward, the board of supervisors, had scheduled a meeting for that same evening to consider public school appropriations for 1955–1956.

The board met a few hours after news of the Supreme Court ruling had been received. Several hundred angry white citizens appeared before it to ask that the proposed school budget not be approved. They urged that the county give up public education rather than undertake to integrate its schools. Grimly, the supervisors voted unanimously to cut off all funds for the operation of public schools.

In my talk with Dowell Howard in May, 1954, he made a wise remark, which has come back to me many times since. "We can do this thing," the Superintendent of Public Instruction said, "if we can avoid *sensations*." Alas, here was a major "sensation" within hours after the announcement of the Supreme Court's 1955 ruling!

The news flashed across the nation, and Prince Edward at once became famous, in a sense which was tragic for the little county, for Virginia, and for the South. Prince Edward became a symbol of the application of the Supreme Court ruling to an "impossible" situation, and an early symbol of resistance to it.

A mass meeting on June 7, attended by some 1,300 citizens, applauded the action of the county's governing board and set about forming an organization and raising a fund to provide private schools for the county's white children. The specific initial purpose was to raise $212,830 to cover the salaries of the sixty-three white teachers for the coming year and to assure their retention. Within a few weeks about three-fourths of this amount had been subscribed.

Upon the advice of state authorities, and being convinced that desegregation would not be required for another year, the Prince Edward County Board reconsidered its action a few weeks later and resumed public school appropriations, though on a month-to-month basis. Nevertheless, the private school organization retained its stand-by nucleus, and the county remained in a posture, thus dramatically demonstrated, of no schools rather than integrated schools.

This "sensation" in Prince Edward and the continuing threat of desegregation orders in that county did much to strengthen and solidify resistance sentiment in Virginia during the following year. It established in many minds the image of a Draconian command from the Supreme Court for sweeping desegregation forthwith in the Black Belt and everywhere else. It was to this fantasy, sedulously cultivated by segregationist agitators, that much of the hostility developed.

The Prince Edward County story, however, is in many respects detached from the larger story of massive resistance. That county proceeded on a basis of complete resistance before any such attitude had been assumed by Virginia. It took steps to close its public schools before school-closing laws were seriously considered by the state; and when, three years later, schools were closed by the state in Warren County, Charlottesville and Norfolk, Prince Edward's public schools were still in full operation. When at last the peremptory desegregation order came in Prince Edward, the state's school-closing laws had been invalidated and all closed schools elsewhere had been reopened. Prince Edward County's public schools were closed in 1959 by action of its own board of supervisors. Even the state's provision for tuition grants to aid pupils attending private schools was rejected in that county. Prince Edward went its own unhappy way.

4. THE GRAY PLAN

IN LATER months and years, as Virginia moved on to far more reckless measures of resistance than the Gray Plan, moderates were to look back upon that program with a certain ironic nostalgia. But in mid-November, 1955, when the Gray Commission at last concluded its labors and submitted its report, its proposals were considered extreme, not only by national observers, but by many Virginians.

The Commission's basic recommendations were three: (1) a system of tuition grants from public funds to aid children who might attend private schools as an escape from public school integration; (2) a locally administered pupil assignment plan, which, though based on criteria other than race, was calculated to keep to a minimum the enrollment of Negroes in white schools; and (3) amendment of the compulsory attendance law to provide that no child could be required to attend an integrated school. Significantly, the assignment plan proposal contemplated local option, and not a uniform policy in all sections to be laid down by the state. The assignment plan itself was acceptable to moderate elements at the time, and the principle later became a prime objective of moderate forces in Virginia.

It was over the tuition grant plan that controversy raged, and the necessity of amending the Virginia constitution before this could be adopted brought the issue immediately before the voters. The proposal was that public funds would be made available, on the one hand, to all children in a locality choosing to close its public schools, or, on the other hand, to any child whose parents rejected integration in a locality which might choose to operate integrated schools. In a test case the Virginia Supreme Court of Appeals had ruled that such payments to students attending private institutions were in violation of Section 141 of the state constitution.

State Senator Gray, who had striven for a report which all, or nearly all, of the Commission's members would sign, did not personally concur in its more moderate recommendations. Two other members signed supplementary statements saying that the proposals did not go far enough in resistance to desegregation. But most members of the Byrd organization greeted the report with enthusiasm.

"I concur wholeheartedly," Governor Stanley said, "in the recommendations from this able, conscientious and dedicated group of legislators."

Byrd himself reserved comment, though the Gray Commission and the legislature, which was about to embrace the first step in the Gray Plan with alacrity, were both dominated by Byrd men.

The Commission had recommended that the Governor set in motion the chain of events necessary to amend Section 141 of the constitution. This Stanley moved swiftly to do. The General Assembly was called in special session November 30. The matter was considered one of the utmost urgency. In a four-day session, acting with near unanimity, the legislature ordered a referendum election for January 9, 1956, on the question of calling a constitutional convention to amend Section 141 so as to permit the adoption of the tuition grant plan.

The five weeks' electoral contest which this move precipitated was one of the most heated in modern Virginia history. To the surprise of many, the apprehensions of the public were in marked contrast to the enthusiasm of political leaders for the tuition grant plan. A very large number of citizens was far from willing to embark upon a program which seemed to jeopardize public education merely to prevent some degree of school integration. The *Richmond Times Dispatch* said on December 18: "If the referendum were held tomorrow, the outcome would be in grave doubt."

The Byrd organization suddenly found itself not leading a stampede, as some apparently had expected, but fighting with its back to the wall. Its own tradition of invincibility was actually at stake. Hence officeholders, former officeholders and all the resources of that famous political organization were mobilized with a thoroughness never before equaled.

Pitted against this powerful force was a relatively unorganized and poorly financed opposition, centralized in a "Society for the Preservation of Public Schools." The Society had a dynamic leader in Delegate and State Senator-elect Armistead L. Boothe, of Alexandria, who was one of the five members of the House of Delegates to vote against the referendum. Boothe was ably assisted by half a dozen liberal politicians, but for the most part the opposition was led by public-spirited amateurs. Three church publications, the *Baptist Religious Herald*, the *Virginia Methodist Advocate* and the *Presbyterian Outlook* were against the tuition grant plan, and many clergymen joined in statements opposing it.

But not all moderates were against the proposal, or against the "Gray Plan," as the question at issue was generally called during the campaign. The question with them was in large part one of how much allowance would have to be made for race prejudice in Virginia in order to keep the public school system intact. Two distinguished educators, Colgate W. Darden, Jr., president of the University of Virginia, and Dr. Dabney S. Lancaster, a former state superintendent of public instruction, espoused the tuition grant plan. Both of these were familiar from personal association with the intense race feeling in Southside Virginia. Dr. Lancaster became a key figure in the pre-convention campaign, directing the "State Referendum Information Center," as its campaign headquarters in Richmond was called. Delegate Robert Whitehead, the acknowledged leader of the anti-Byrd-machine faction in the General Assembly, separated himself from many liberal former associates to endorse the tuition grant plan. All three of these acted on assurances that the Gray Plan would embrace local option; all three later were to oppose massive resistance.

The extreme segregationists were almost without exception in favor of the tuition grant plan, and the greatest effort was made to bring out the vote in Southside Virginia. In that sensitive area campaigners presented the complicated matter as a simple question of school segregation. Handbills read: "Remember a vote for the convention is a vote against enforced mixed schools."

In the northern and western half of the state the campaign took a different tone. Here many of the rank and file were induced to vote for tuition grants by the promise of local option. Although only the tuition grant proposal was at issue in the referendum, campaign literature in these sections reminded the voters that "the Gray Commission recognizes the varying conditions throughout the Commonwealth by giving the greatest amount of local option to meet these conditions. It recognizes the Supreme Court decision by permitting school integration in communities that choose that course, but prevents enforced integration."

On December 18 Senator Byrd issued a statement saying that he would vote for the calling of a constitutional convention, but adding: "I am not commenting on the other features of the Gray report." In a conference with trusted leaders of his organization in his office in Washington he confided that he had other plans in mind which should have priority over the Gray program, and decreed that the local option feature of the Gray Plan should be scuttled altogether. It remained, nevertheless, supremely important for the organization's prestige that the referendum election should be won, and Byrd's followers redoubled their efforts to this end.

On January 9, when the votes were counted, 304,154 had voted in favor of a constitutional convention; 144,000 had voted "No." In Southside Virginia, where the heaviest vote was cast, the vote was four to one in favor of calling the convention. In western Virginia relatively few went to the polls. A substantial number had voted for a feature of the Gray Plan which was not printed on the ballot, and which was about to be discarded: local option.

5. INTERPOSITION

THE GRAY PLAN forces were jubilant. "It's like we'd won the War Between the States!" Gray exclaimed. But Gray and most of his associates did not interpret the results of the January 9 referendum as a victory for the actual Gray Commission recommendations; they hailed them simply as a mandate from the people for the utmost resistance to school integration.

Merging opportunely also with the belated frown of Senator Byrd to cause the derailment of the relatively moderate Gray

Plan was a thing called "interposition." Discovered—or disinterred—by an elderly country lawyer named William Olds, interposition was the doctrine once held in one form or another by Southern leaders that a state had a right to "interpose its sovereignty" between the federal government and its people. Olds (who was later honored for this accomplishment by being named a circuit court judge) put his findings into a pamphlet, which came to the attention of the *Richmond News Leader*.

The *News Leader*, which greeted the Supreme Court ruling of May, 1954, with a conciliatory editorial and a suggested program of compliance, had changed quickly to an attitude of fierce hostility. By October, 1955, it had become probably the most resounding voice of resistance in the Southern press. This paper, long distinguished by the scholarly editorials of the late Douglas Southall Freeman, biographer of Lee and Washington, had been edited since 1951 by a dynamic former reporter named James Jackson Kilpatrick, Jr. "Jack" Kilpatrick was thirty-one years of age when he succeeded to Dr. Freeman's editorial chair. A native of Oklahoma, he had succeeded in becoming somewhat "more Virginian than Virginia."

To this zealous resister, groping for a formula, Olds' paper was pure gold. He seized upon the idea and went to work in the spirit of a man with a historic mission. Day after day most of the paper's editorial page was devoted to interposition. The Virginia Resolution of 1798 was reprinted in full, as also the Kentucky Resolutions of 1798 and 1799. Voluminous editorials, written with the solemnity and eloquence of great state papers, appeared daily alongside three-column portraits of Jefferson, Madison, Calhoun and other pre-Civil-War immortals. Indubitably this talented young editor would have been a convincing champion of the Southern cause before 1865.

After six weeks, and 50,000 words in the *News Leader*, the

strange new word "interposition" had entered the vocabulary
of most adult Virginians and of politicians all across the South.
Reprints of the interposition editorials had been distributed beyond the *News Leader's* circulation range. A group of extreme
segregationists, meeting in Memphis, Tennessee, urged Virginia to "interpose its sovereignty" when the legislature met
in January and called on all Southern states to fall in line. In
Washington Senator Harry F. Byrd said on the floor of the
Senate: "Mr. Kilpatrick has presented a fine service to the
State of Virginia. . . ."

Before the legislature opened on January 11, the *News
Leader* published a resolution of interposition in proper form
for introduction in that body. There was a great variety of
opinions on the question of how far the document should go
and just how rebellious its language should be. Many strove
anxiously to frame an interposition which would not be nullifi-
cation, although if interposition meant anything it meant just
that. Virginia legislators debated and split hairs for several
weeks. Finally they were able to secure a nearly unanimous
vote for the adoption of a resolution which said in part:

That by its decision of May 17, 1954, in the school cases, the
Supreme Court of the United States placed upon the Constitution
an interpretation, having the effect of an amendment thereto, which
interpretation Virginia emphatically disapproves;

That with the Supreme Court's decision aforesaid and this resolution by the General Assembly of Virginia, a question of contested
power has arisen: The court asserts, for its part, that the States did,
in fact, in 1868, prohibit unto themselves, by means of the Fourteenth Amendment, the power to maintain racially separate public
schools, which power certain of the States have exercised daily for
more than 80 years; the State of Virginia, for her part, asserts that
she has never surrendered such power. . . .

[That Virginia] anxiously concerned at this massive expansion
of central authority . . . is in duty bound to interpose against
these most serious consequences, and earnestly to challenge the

usurped authority that would inflict them upon her citizens. . . .

And be it finally resolved that until the question here asserted by the State of Virginia be settled by clear constitutional amendment, we pledge our firm intention to take all appropriate measures, legally and constitutionally available to us, to resist this illegal encroachment upon our sovereign powers and to urge upon our sister states, whose authorities over their own most cherished powers may next be imperiled, their prompt and deliberate efforts to check this and further encroachment by the Supreme Court, through judicial legislation, upon the reserved powers of the states.

In the meantime the idea had been taken up by the four other Southern states whose legislatures were then in session. Alabama beat Virginia to interposition, with a resolution which declared the Supreme Court decision "null, void, and of no effect."

Senator Byrd, busy with Southern colleagues in Washington in the preparation of an all-Southern resistance gesture, declared:

If we can organize the Southern States for massive resistance to this order, I think that in time the rest of the country will realize that racial integration is not going to be accepted in the South. . . . In interposition, the South has a perfectly legal means of appeal from the Supreme Court's order.

The Gray Plan schedule had been calculated to carry out the constitutional amendment procedure in time for the enactment of implementing legislation before the General Assembly adjourned on March 10. When the constitutional convention met March 5–7 and perfunctorily adopted the Gray Plan amendment, the Gray Plan itself had almost faded from the picture. In a digression of questionable propriety from the official object of its meeting, the constitutional convention commended the Governor and the General Assembly "for their invocation of the historic doctrine of interposition for the preservation of the sovereign rights of this Commonwealth."

The expression "massive resistance" had not yet come into common use; but the principle of massive, or total, resistance had already begun to dominate state policy. That principle in its intra-state application meant above all the denial of local option. It called for uniform resistance to the Supreme Court ruling, whatever the conditions or the sentiment in any particular city or county.

The application of the principle to those localities with a minor race problem which wished to go forward with plans for adjustment to the court's ruling was accurately, if somewhat brutally, described in the exclamation of Congressman William M. Tuck, a former governor and trusted Byrd lieutenant: "If they won't go along with us," Tuck said, "I say make 'em!"

The Supreme Court had remanded the school cases to district courts "because of their proximity to local conditions. . . ." The Court had said: "School authorities have the primary responsibility of elucidating, assessing and solving these problems; courts will have to consider whether the action of school authorities constitutes good faith implementation of the governing constitutional principles."

Virginia had itself urged the desirability of local option in the Supreme Court hearing of April, 1955. Attorney General Almond said to the Court then: "Broad, nondiscriminatory discretion to be exercised without discrimination must be vested in local school boards to cope with varying conditions extant throughout the State."

The Gray Commission had included local option among its recommendations, and its proponents had promised local option in many sections. Now in the glow of interposition, local initiative in solving the desegregation problem suddenly was regarded as something seditious and wicked.

In this atmosphere the legislature learned that the Arlington County school board had drawn up a tentative plan for the desegregation of that county's schools. "Assuming that the Legislature will enact the provisions recommended by the Gray Commission," the Arlington board published the broad outlines of a desegregation program to begin in September, 1956.

The General Assembly swiftly retaliated by taking away from Arlington County its privilege of electing its school board by popular vote. Arlington, having a unique system of local government, was the only county in Virginia where school board members were so elected. The Arlington school board members were required to be appointed thenceforth by the county's governing board.

Most moderates accepted interposition as a harmless gesture. But echoes of the Gray Plan campaign came back to plague the legislators when a resolution was introduced expressing disapproval of any school desegregation steps during the 1956–1957 term. The resolution was introduced by Speaker of the House of Delegates E. Blackburn Moore. Moore, who will appear significantly from time to time in this story of massive resistance, is a neighbor, fellow apple-orchardist and close friend of Senator Byrd.

The resolution aroused bitter opposition in the western part of the state, where the *Roanoke Times* and other newspapers called it "a betrayal," and "a violent contradiction" of promises made. The *Staunton News-Leader* said:

Even the proposal of the resolution has inspired charges of bad faith with the people, who were assured . . . that adoption of the Gray Commission's recommendations would give the localities wide discretion for working out their integration problems, permitting integration by those cities and counties desiring it.

Rather than precipitate an open debate and mar the "harmony" of the session, the Moore resolution was quietly shelved by a Senate committee.

With that, the General Assembly adjourned. Segregationists in Virginia—and over much of the South—hailed the mirage of interposition, and there for the time being the resistance effort in Virginia rested.

6. BYRD'S MASSIVE RESISTANCE

BYRD and his unique political organization had dominated Virginia for over a quarter of a century. Rising liberal opposition at long last had threatened their control in the gubernatorial contests of 1949 and 1953, but once the Byrd-chosen governor was safely elected, the machine's domination was almost complete. The opposition in the legislature was insignificant and nearly all public offices throughout the state were filled by loyal followers of the Senator.

Harry Byrd, the heavy-set, well-dressed, gentlemanly "Senator's Senator," with ruddy cheeks and vigorous step—reflecting outdoor life at his apple orchards—and almost cherubic features, bore little resemblance to the usual conception of the political boss; but few political bosses in the United States had held such power or wielded it as long as he. The "organization," dignified, respectable, deriving much of its strength from its long record of conservative, frugal and notably honest management of the state's business, was an institution unique in American politics. Byrd's fame stems in the first instance from a remarkable and never-to-be-forgotten performance as governor (1926–1930). He enjoyed in Virginia an almost mystical prestige; and his hold over the organization itself was such that eager politicians took their cue from the Senator's slightest hint, or sought to fathom his wishes when express directions were lacking. After his initial statement in May, 1954, Byrd was almost silent on the subject of the Supreme Court ruling for over a year. But his feeling was well known to the political confraternity: he resented it from the depths of his soul.

It was not primarily a matter of race prejudice with Byrd. Although his organization was strongest in Southside Virginia, he himself resided in a northwestern corner of the state, where Negroes were rare. White supremacy had never been conspicuous in Byrd's philosophy. He was never regarded as "anti-Negro." He still liked to recall that as governor he secured the enactment in 1926 of "the strongest anti-lynching law that has ever been enacted," and he pointed with pride to the fact that "since that date, Virginia has not had a single lynching."

But Byrd gloried in the story of Virginia's post-Civil-War "redemption" from carpetbagger rule, and a passionate and lifelong attachment to the principle of state rights permeated his very being. One may suspect, too, a certain feeling that, in ordering an end to a time-honored practice in Virginia, the Supreme Court had intruded, not merely upon the rights of states, but upon the personal domain of Harry Byrd.

Byrd was never publicly identified with the Gray Plan, apart from his statement issued to the press in mid-campaign, confirming his support of the proposal to call a constitutional convention. At that hectic stage of the vote-getting effort, his press release, which was of doubtful value as campaign material, was published only in part and attracted little attention. Surprisingly to the fast-moving Gray Plan promoters, he said: "I trust Virginia will take adequate time to feel our way along."

Ten other states [the Senator added] are confronted with the same acute problem. These states are all seeking a way to preserve their schools, and it is possible that some form of action can be accepted as a pattern for all.

As developments occur, and the resistance of the South continues, it is possible, I believe, that there can be some degree of coalition between the 11 Southern States which will strengthen the position of the individual state.

In a note of hysteria, not conducive to any rational approach to the problem, Byrd also said: "Some believe that the Washington Court will begin to fine and imprison school officials in Virginia next September unless integration is in operation throughout the State."

The Byrd machine campaigners fought for the Gray Plan constitutional amendment until the referendum election was won, then they turned to interposition. Byrd in Washington was now engrossed in a movement to unite the representatives of Southern states in a solemn declaration of defiance of the Supreme Court's ruling. On March 12, 1956, the Southern Manifesto, signed by 101 Southern members, was duly introduced in the House and Senate—"a part," Byrd said, "of the plan of massive resistance we've been working on and I hope and believe it will be an effective action."

Summer came and neither interposition nor the Southern Manifesto had greatly changed the situation. Six states had now "interposed their sovereignty," but interposition no longer made sensational news. Virginia's brave resolution, which had been forwarded to each member of the Supreme Court and of the Congress, languished in neglected files.

For its part, the National Association for the Advancement of Colored People seemed only spurred to greater activity. Suits seeking to end racial segregation in the schools by the start of the fall term had been filed against school boards of four localities, Arlington County, Norfolk, Newport News and Charlottesville, in addition to the long-standing suit against that of Prince Edward County, which was scheduled for a hearing on July 9.

It was clear now that massive resistance would have to be spelled out in more specific legislation if, under court pressure, a solid front of segregation was to be maintained throughout the commonwealth. On July 2 Governor Stanley, State Senator Gray and other trusted leaders of the organization met with Byrd in his Washington office. There, in an unpublicized conference, this powerful group decided to go all the way. They determined to secure legislation which would make the integration of any public school in Virginia virtually impossible. Returning to Richmond, Governor Stanley called the General Assembly to meet in special session on August 27.

By now, the public, which had hesitated to embrace the relatively moderate Gray Commission proposals nine months earlier, had been conditioned for the utmost in reckless defiance. The flood of political oratory, the inflammatory editorials and the bold words from respected leaders had done their work. Extremists were in the ascendancy, and not only "integrationist," but "moderate" had become a term of reproach.

7. A VERY SPECIAL SESSION

To PREPARE the reader for the extraordinary legislation which came out of that 1956 special session of the Virginia General Assembly it is necessary to picture the setting and the atmosphere in which that body met.

Two days earlier Byrd, addressing a large gathering at his apple orchards at Berryville, had wished the Governor "much success" in the impending session, and said of the Supreme Court ruling: "Let Virginia surrender to this illegal demand and you'll find the ranks of the South broken. . . . If Virginia surrenders, the rest of the South will go down too."

In the historic capital of the Southern Confederacy, 100 miles south of Washington and the Supreme Court, crowds filled the galleries of the House of Delegates on the morning of August 27, and Confederate flags fluttered.

The gallery contingent came largely in answer to the call of a propaganda sheet circulated widely in the area of Virginia where Negroes are most numerous and where race prejudice is greatest. It carried a Confederate soldier at its masthead and was called the *Virginian*. This special issue of the *Virginian* carried a page of dubious photographs depicting "integration as it really is"—from white and Negro children mingling on the playground to a white woman lying across a bed with a repulsive Negro man.

"Let fathers and mothers travel to the capital," the *Virginian* said, "and see the fate of our children decided. . . . Let Virginians from every crossroad and byway, journey to Richmond on this day of days."

The members of the Virginia legislature are on the whole gentlemen of education and refinement, perhaps above the average for state legislators. In ordinary times these state senators and delegates would have consigned such trash to the waste baskets. But today most of them had the *Virginian* spread over their desks or carried it conspicuously in side coat pockets.

The *Virginian* also displayed a large drawing of Patrick Henry in an oratorical pose with the caption:

"In 1775 Virginia was threatened by a tyrant; but Virginia had a man to answer him, PATRICK HENRY. . . . Will we, in our time, fight Tyranny? Or will we crawl—and bring eternal disgrace to our names and to our native soil?"

The Governor's message was more dignified, but it was in the same spirit. Stanley was a tall, well-heeled furniture manufacturer and former Congressman of sixty-six, whose normally affable personality was little suited to high drama. His strained, plaintive voice hardly fitted his rhetorical questions:

"Do we accept the attempt of the Supreme Court of the United States to dictate administration of our internal affairs?"

"Do we accept integration?"

But the "No's" from the two chambers in joint session were rugged enough.

The key measure in the thirteen-bill anti-integration package presented to the legislature, and the issue which furnished the effective test of strength between the extremists and the local option forces, was the Governor's so-called "cut-off-the-funds" proposal, which was House Bill No. 1. Stanley had announced in July his intention to request the General Assembly to cut off state school funds from any district in which any public school should be integrated, and this threat had already been the subject of heated controversy. (Over the state as a whole, 42 per cent of the cost of operating schools is borne by the state.) In the form in which the bill came to a vote in the legislature it had been modulated to the extent that it denied state school funds only to the elementary schools, or only to the secondary schools, of a district, if integration should be limited to schools in only one of these categories.

In spite of the atmosphere of noisy defiance, the legislators were far from unanimous in this initial test of their willingness to embark upon a drastic program of resistance to the Supreme Court ruling. The bill received sixty-one to thirty-seven votes in the House of Delegates, but it passed the Senate by only a narrow margin. Twenty-one senators voted for, and seventeen against the bill. One senator, who was absent because of sickness, let it be known that he would have attended the session and cast a negative vote if his vote would have been the deciding factor. It is pertinent to an appraisal of the basic popular support for massive resistance in Virginia that the twenty-one senators who favored the bill represented districts containing less than a majority of the people of Virginia. They represented little more than one million of the state's 2,581,555 white persons (by the 1950 census). Fourteen of the twenty-one were from overrepresented constituencies of Southside Virginia. Needless to say, the state's Negroes were opposed to the legislation with virtual unanimity.

In the twenty-seven-day session, a total of twenty-three acts were passed dealing with the school segregation issue or aimed at the NAACP. The greater part of the session's oratory and contention had to do with House Bill No. 1. Much less attention was given to a more fateful measure. A bill which rendered the provisions for cutting off school funds almost academic was enacted with little debate and much confusion. This bill had never been printed, and few legislators could say at the time in precisely what form it passed. It was a lengthy document, setting forth many procedures calculated to discourage Negroes from applying, or from persisting in their applications, for enrollment in white schools. It provided for the compensation of the principals and teachers of closed schools and for assistance to displaced pupils in attending private schools. But the heart of the bill was the blunt command that in the event of the enrollment of any child in a school of another race, "such school is closed and removed from the public school system. . . ."

Hatred of the NAACP had reached a high pitch in Virginia. It was shared in varying degrees by many who accepted the inevitability of gradual compliance with the desegregation ruling. The bitterness was reflected, during this September special session, in seven different acts intended to investigate, embarrass, curb or cripple the NAACP in this state. Registration was required of groups financing lawsuits to which they were not a party and of groups engaged in activities on behalf of any particular race; sundry presumably embarrassing information was required to be furnished; punishment was prescribed for initiating lawsuits in various specified circumstances; and two investigating committees were set up.

A word should be said here about the moderates in the General Assembly. For moderates there were, and liberals—an anxious, suffering, vainly struggling, courageous group. The problem which confronted the moderate minority on the race question in Virginia, as elsewhere in the South, was both painful and infinitely complicated. In a legislative body where the extremist majority was in an emotional and vindictive mood, the moderate member needed constantly to weigh the satisfaction of frank expression of his views against his practical usefulness as a legislator. Outspoken opposition to anti-integration measures could narrowly limit his circle of friends, exclude him from important committee assignments, and deny him cooperation even in legislative undertakings having no relation to the segregation issue.

But moderate legislators did speak out against the tragic folly of Virginia's massive resistance legislation. Delegate Robert Whitehead had opposed the interposition resolution in the regular session in one of the most eloquent and scholarly speeches heard in the state's legislature in recent years. Mrs. Kathryn Stone, a gracious and indomitable lady member of the House of Delegates, opposed resistance in most trying circumstances and at every step. Two major political figures, Democratic State Senator Armistead L. Boothe and Republican State Senator Ted Dalton, working as a team, made a valiant last-ditch fight for local option in the September session. Most moderates, while standing firm on crucial issues, sought to conserve their influence by joining in criticism of the Supreme Court and insisting that integration should be held to a minimum.

A few, like Mrs. Stone, Delegate John Webb, State Senator Stuart B. Carter, and State Senator (former Richmond Mayor) Edward E. Haddock, expressed their disapproval of resistance chicanery without reserve. When the seven anti-NAACP bills passed the House of Delegates, opposing votes never numbered more than nine in that 100-member body. Only three members opposed all seven bills; they were Mrs. Stone, Delegate Webb and Delegate Vernon S. Shaffer, one of the lonely Republican members. For anyone in public life in Virginia to say frankly that race segregation was wrong was almost unheard of. Carter's performance was probably unique when on September 20 he declared on the floor of the Virginia State Senate: "I do conscientiously believe in integration." One needs to be familiar with the odium which has become attached to the word "integration" in the South to realize how much courage that affirmation required.

Leading the extremist majority, and riding on top of the emotional wave, were some of the most potent figures in the Byrd organization. State Senator Mills E. Godwin was chairman of the massive resistance team. Godwin aptly voiced the prevailing hostility to the principle of local option when he said the program was "needed as a deterrent to those localities in Virginia which have, or may indicate, a willingness to integrate." State Senator Gray was now in the forefront of the opposition to local option and an advocate of resistance to the utmost. State Senator Harry Byrd, Jr., and Speaker of the House Moore, his neighbor and a bosom friend of the elder Byrd, were closely associated in furthering the massive resistance cause. Delegate James M. Thomson, a brother of Mrs.

Harry Byrd, Jr., and an intransigent racist, was a leader of the most fanatic segregationists throughout the massive resistance era. Thomson sponsored one of the bills creating an investigating committee; and later, as chairman of his committee, he was to shock many, including federal courts, by arrogant harassment of the NAACP and some of its liberal friends.

There were many complications in the school-closing legislation which we need not examine here, beyond noting one tiny loophole through which, in the Governor's discretion and entirely from local funds, a district might conceivably operate an integrated school. The Governor could permit this, if he should deem it advisable, upon joint petition of the school board and the governing body of the locality affected. Cautious proponents of this provision reasoned that the massive resistance legislation would stand a better chance of surviving court test if it stopped barely short of total prohibition of racial integration.

Another act, which was to be much haggled over later in the courts and in the legislature, vested the authority for the assignment of all pupils to public schools in Virginia in a State Pupil Placement Board, which, it was clearly understood, would assign no Negro to any white school.

The last loophole, it was believed, had been plugged. Virginia dug itself in behind the battlements of massive resistance and waited for the attack.

8. VOICES CRYING IN THE WILDERNESS

IN FEBRUARY, 1955, a Virginia Council on Human Relations had been formed to promote friendship between the races and "reduce race tension, racial misunderstanding and racial distrust." The first president of the group was the Reverend Carroll Brooke, an Episcopal minister, of Staunton, who was also head of the Department of Christian Social Relations of the Virginia Council of Churches. The first full-time executive secretary of the Council on Human Relations, when it opened an office in Richmond, was Reverend John H. Marion, a Presbyterian minister. The Virginia Council, like Councils on Human Relations in other Southern states, was affiliated with the Southern Regional Council, an organization of liberal Southerners from thirteen states, with headquarters in Atlanta.

Both of the officers mentioned were white, but the Virginia Council's members were about equally divided between white and Negro citizens and Negroes took a prominent part in its activities. A number of other organizations in the state, in addition to church bodies, consistently favored compliance with the desegregation ruling. The list included the American Association of University Women, Leagues of Women Voters, several Jewish organizations and the Virginia branch of the AFL-CIO. But only the Council on Human Relations was substantially interracial in composition and wholly devoted to the fight against race discrimination. It advocated not only desegregation, but tolerance and equality of opportunity in the whole field of interracial relations.

Such an organization would not have been popular in Virginia at any time. In the emotional climate of the massive resistance era it was viewed in many quarters with suspicion,

hostility or contempt. Nevertheless, it rallied a handful of dedicated people, and grew in three years to a total membership of
some 1,500, with half a dozen local chapters in Virginia cities.

On the Negro side, the Council's membership was eminently
representative of the minority race. Negro college presidents
and professors, Negro lawyers and clergymen and other prominent Negroes were active in it. Its white members, on the
other hand, were exceptional, rather than representative. They
were an earnest, unselfish and courageous group, with clergymen prominent among them, but they included virtually none
of the economic or political power structure of the state.

Within those limitations, the Council on Human Relations
provided a continuous and valuable channel of interracial communication. Its anti-segregation message also was carried to the
public in reports of distinguished speakers at its meetings, in
its own public statements, in the press and in the activities of
its individual members. It stirred the conscience of many Virginians; and its objectives were shared by a considerably larger
number than, in the existing atmosphere, were willing to enroll in it.

In April, 1955, one political group had taken a surprisingly
emphatic position in favor of compliance with the Supreme
Court's decision. The executive committee of the Young Republican Federation, meeting in Richmond then, adopted a
resolution which said:

"We believe . . . in the Supreme Court as the highest authority to interpret the Constitution, [and] oppose any attempt to circumvent or violate the Constitution by legal or
quasi-legal devices."

That went farther than any Republican body was prepared
to go again, and some Republicans were among the most uncompromising segregationists. But the Republican Party remained predominantly the moderate party on this issue in Vir-

ginia. Its leader, State Senator Ted Dalton, who had come sensationally close to winning the governorship in 1953, was one of the few legislators who had consistently opposed the massive resistance laws. He was to run for governor again in 1957, on a moderate platform.

The Richmond First Club is an organization of public-spirited business and professional men which concerns itself actively, but on a non-partisan basis, with the public affairs of that city. Its influence is normally substantial when it takes a position upon questions of municipal policy.

In the summer of 1955, when rational discussion of public school desegregation was still permissible, the Richmond First Club appointed a committee of five to study the problem as it affected the capital city. R. Hugh Rudd, Jr., an attorney, was chairman of the group; the other members were J. Edwin Du-Priest, Irving I. Held. Richard N. Smith, Jr., and Merritt I. Taylor.

The committee labored quietly for six months, apparently unperturbed by the din of the Gray Plan campaign and the fevered oratory of the legislative session. Then on February 23, 1956, it reported its finding: it concluded that integration of the public schools of Richmond could proceed smoothly if parents and officials would resolve to make it work.

The report reviewed the experience of five cities where schools had been integrated: Dover, Delaware; Evansville, Indiana; St. Louis, Missouri; Baltimore, Maryland; and Washington, D. C. It noted that in Baltimore only 3 per cent of the Negro students entered formerly all white schools. In the large-scale integration operation in Washington it observed that "the issue of segregation or integration was quickly lost in the over-riding issue of how best to maintain the standards of education."

It quoted the Dover Superintendent of Schools as saying:

"The plan has worked very well to date and has provided' a pilot group who, as the program is broadened, will help the adjustment of the others that will follow." An Evansville school official was quoted as saying: "Our experience has been very satisfactory and accompanied by a minimum of unpleasantness."

From the St. Louis experience the committee noted that when optional integration takes place in high schools as many as one-third of the Negroes eligible may choose to remain in their old schools. It added that the influence of churches, civic and school groups and the newspapers, "combined with the natural respect for law on the part of the majority of its citizens, was sufficient in St. Louis, as we believe it would be sufficient in most American cities, to create a climate of friendliness and good will in which desegregation might take place."

All this and more of the report was fairly and adequately presented in the editorially hostile press. But seldom has so precious a document been so quickly consigned to oblivion as was the Richmond First Club committee's report. Had its authors been politicians, they would undoubtedly have been pilloried for their patriotism. Had they been citizens of less prestige, they might have been attacked. The report was fiercely ignored. The still small voice was lost in the din of interposition and massive resistance.

The strongest influence for moderation in Virginia was that of the clergymen. Though few of them spoke out openly on the subject as individuals, when the question was raised in state or district meetings a majority were invariably ready to take a position on the side of compliance with the Supreme Court ruling. Nothing so stern and forthright had been heard from the clergy, however, as the 1,500-word statement issued by the Richmond Ministers' Association in January, 1957.

Without mincing words these ministers denounced the "ineptitude" of the state's massive resistance legislation and the legislators' "strange persistence, compounded with pride, prejudice and personal bitterness toward persons of opposite opinions."

"The present Governor and a majority of the Legislature," the statement said, "have, in our opinion, seriously impaired the sacred and historic traditions of Virginia democracy and lowered the prestige of the State in the eyes of thoughtful people."

The incident, including a poll of ministers not present at the meeting (which confirmed majority endorsement of it), was fairly reported in the press, but in their editorial columns both Richmond newspapers reproached and ridiculed the city's clergymen.

9. THE RISE OF LINDSAY ALMOND

IN THE legislative alarums and excursions over the desegregation problem thus far, State Attorney General J. Lindsay Almond, Jr., had played a cooperative rather than a positive role. None of the steps taken by the General Assembly were suggested by him; in fact, he gave evidence of being skeptical of some of them. But he yielded to no one in his attachment to the principle of segregation, and now that he was free from the inhibitions of a lawyer pleading before the Supreme Court, no one could match the purple eloquence of his tirades against that high tribunal.

At one point Almond's seeming lack of enthusiasm for the existing resistance posture led to a taunt from Byrd's trusted lieutenant, Blackburn Moore. On June 1, 1956, the Speaker of the House of Delegates said in a public statement:

"I ask the Attorney General to inform the people of Virginia . . . whether he proposes to fight for a continuance of segregated schools . . . or does he desire legislation that would permit any form of integration for this coming year?"

Almond was "shocked at the unwarranted and unjustified attack." "For more than five years I have fought with my back to the wall," he retorted. "I have exhausted every legal defense. . . . Throughout this long, heart-rending struggle, not one suggestion has come from Mr. Moore. . . ."

Moore's statement was plainly intended as a trial balloon, and as a brake on Almond's unannounced campaign for governor —an office for which the Speaker himself was sometimes considered. But nobody joined in the attack on the Attorney General.

Lindsay Almond had been plodding steadily toward the governorship since he left a seat in Congress to run for state attorney general in 1948. A stout, white-haired orator of the old school, with a great deal of natural independence, Almond little resembled the suave, disciplined politicians in gray flannel suits generally associated with the Byrd machine. He never felt completely at home with the machine leaders, nor they with him, although he scrupulously followed the organization line and sought to integrate himself in that powerful group. His greatest political asset was his ability to impress crowds of ordinary people—a talent of which Byrd and his associates were instinctively suspicious.

As state attorney general, Almond had argued the case of Prince Edward County during the long litigation leading to the Supreme Court's rulings of 1954 and 1955, and he was for several years the state's outstanding and most publicized defender of segregation. After the 1955 ruling there were many to challenge his primacy as the segregationist hero. But, with his easy eloquence and tireless speechmaking, the Attorney General had continued to grow in popularity among politicians of the lower echelon and with the rank and file of voters.

Nineteen fifty-seven was the year for the election of a governor in Virginia. Although formal announcements of candidacy are not usually made until the beginning of the election year, it is customary for jockeying for place among aspirants to begin many months earlier. It is also customary for anyone hopeful of receiving Senator Byrd's nod of approval to discuss the matter with him before announcing his candidacy. No one has been elected governor of Virginia in the past thirty years without Byrd's endorsement, or at least (as in one case) Byrd's acquiescence.

That Lindsay Almond had his eye on the governorship had long been well known. No one else had conducted what could be called a campaign; but Byrd and his inner circle of politicians were still toying with the idea of putting forward a more congenial candidate. State Senator Gray, for instance, was more to Byrd's liking, and Gray was more than willing. But Almond, with an air of complete confidence, continued to shake hands, button-hole friends and make speeches in every section of the state.

Suddenly, on November 17, Almond formally declared himself a candidate for governor of Virginia. From the lower and middle levels of machine stalwarts a stream of endorsements at once began to pour in; but from the top leaders there were two weeks of silence. Those gentlemen scurried back and forth and conferred anxiously, while Gray hurriedly appraised his own strength. Finally they reached the obvious conclusion that Almond could not be beaten, and that to try to beat him would be disastrous. Byrd himself, returning from a hunting trip in Canada, concurred. So they clasped Almond to their bosom.

The signal came in an announcement from Gray on December 6 that in order to prevent "a division among the proponents of segregated schools" he would not oppose Almond. The Attorney General, Gray said, had been "prominent among those who have striven to prevent integration, which most Virginians abhor. . . ."

Byrd himself, five days later, accepting the Attorney General's nomination as a foregone conclusion, called for an all-out effort for a sweeping Democratic victory in the general election, and said:

"In Lindsay Almond the Democratic Party will have a candidate tried and tested by many years of arduous public service. . . ."

Almond eagerly took on his shoulders the Byrd machine and all its works, including the whole spate of massive resistance laws. He had no serious opposition in the Democratic primary, in which he received all but a handful of the votes cast; but the general election was hotly contested.

The platform of the Democratic candidates for governor, lieutenant governor and attorney general read in part:

We will oppose with every faculty at our command, and with every ounce of our energy, the attempt to mix white and Negro races in our classrooms. Let there be no misunderstanding, no weasel words on this point. . . . We will not yield as long as a single avenue of resistance remains unexplored.

Theodore Roosevelt (rarely called other than "Ted") Dalton was the strongest leader the Virginia Republican Party had developed since the nineteenth century. He had received a phenomenal 45 per cent of the vote when he ran for governor in 1953. In 1957 he was under heavy pressure to make the race again. Dalton was opposed to massive resistance, although he favored as much public school segregation as could be legally retained. He stood above all for local option and open schools.

Finally prevailed upon to accept another Republican nomination for governor, he announced: "I shall in a calm, clear voice tell the great people of Virginia that the 'cut-off-the-funds, close-the-schools' policy of the Democratic machine will bring chaos to our public school system."

A tall, blond, jovial extrovert, Dalton enjoyed immense personal popularity in Virginia, and his integrity and unusual ability were nowhere questioned. The Democratic and pro-massive-resistance *Richmond Times-Dispatch* said of the two candidates:

Between J. Lindsay Almond, Jr. . . . and Ted Dalton, Virginians will choose for governor one of two men intimately familiar with the state's government and each thoroughly capable of presiding over this commonwealth in a manner to reflect credit on themselves and the state.

However, as the campaign took shape, the moderate Republican was labeled "integrationist," and all who believed in segregation were urged to vote for Almond. The latter campaigned with a kind of ferocity, mainly against the NAACP, the Supreme Court and the federal government. His reckless fulminations aroused fears in many quarters that he was planting the seeds of future violence.

Dalton and Horace Henderson, the able and indefatigable Republican candidate for lieutenant governor, launched a vigorous campaign based on a hope that the moderate element was at last ready to rebel against the disastrous trend in state policy on the school segregation issue. If there had been any possibility of such an upsurge, it vanished quickly when federal troops took over the school situation in Little Rock,

Arkansas. The shock of that incident, which was exploited to the full by the Democratic campaigners, had a devastating effect upon the Republican effort in Virginia.

Almond boasted again and again that under massive resistance "no schools have been closed and no integration has taken place." Though he did not promise it definitely, when the campaign was over the Democratic candidate had given the impression to thousands that, in some unexplained way, he would preserve both segregation and public education in Virginia. On that proposition, Virginia gave him 63 per cent of its popular vote.

Almond's inaugural address on January 11, 1958 in parts was not unlike the message of a chief executive about to lead his nation to war against a foreign foe. Scattered whoops, whistles and rebel yells came more and more frequently as he warmed to his oratorical offensive. He ridiculed the proposal that each locality should be left free to decide for itself. He called upon the General Assembly "to stand firm with unfailing unity of purpose and high resolve against every assault upon the sovereignty of this commonwealth."

"Against these massive attacks," he said, "we must marshal a massive resistance."

Ironically, as it seems in retrospect, the new Governor said: "And to paraphrase a great statesman, I say to you that I have not been elected governor to preside over the liquidation of Virginia's public schools."

Inauguration Day in Richmond is always a happy occasion for Senator Byrd. Each quadrennial inauguration of a governor means one more problem solved and one more state administration launched with the Senator's blessing. The festive gathering gives him a rare opportunity to greet old friends and admiring followers from all sections of Virginia. Byrd had campaigned for Almond (though primarily for massive resistance), and Almond's inauguration day was no exception. Byrd beamed with satisfaction and bonhomie as he mingled with the crowd in the state capitol. Though the Senator had turned seventy the previous June, he was in vigorous health, and his cheeks were never rosier.

As usual, Byrd fraternized cordially with his fellow former governors, of whom, in addition to retiring Governor Stanley, three were present: Colgate W. Darden, Jr., president of the University of Virginia; John S. Battle, then a member of the Civil Rights Commission; and Congressman William M. Tuck. Though uniformly devoted to Byrd, these varied in their attitudes toward massive resistance.

A reporter approached each of the four former governors and asked what he thought of Almond's inaugural address. The four replies were significant:

Darden: "Very interesting."

Battle: "A very fine speech."

Tuck: "One of the finest speeches I ever heard."

Byrd: "One of the most notable speeches ever delivered in Virginia."

The session of the legislature from early January to early March, 1958, was uneventful in comparison to recent previous sessions. Anti-integration sentiment was stronger than ever, but there seemed to be little that could be added to the collection of massive resistance laws already on the statute books. There were, however, the "Little Rock Bills." Indignation over the use of federal troops at Little Rock found expression in an act requiring the closing of any school which might be policed by federal troops, and another act authorizing the governor to extend such closing to all other schools in the affected district. The object of the second act was to assure the closing of Negro schools as well as white schools in such a contingency.

The most exciting event of the session was the announcement by Byrd on February 12 that he would not be a candidate for re-election to the United States Senate the following November. Although not a matter of official concern to the General Assembly, this became for two weeks the intense preoccupation of that body.

The outpouring of eulogies of the Senator by his admirers in the legislature was unprecedented in modern Virginia. Governor Almond himself visited the state Senate to add his voice to the rest. The effusions could hardly have been very different had the news told of the Senator's death. State Senator Mills E. Godwin said mournfully, as if standing over the uncovered bier: "We shall never look upon his like again." State Senator Harry Byrd, Jr., witnessing the outpouring of tributes to his father, said in a voice husky with emotion that he wished his mother and two brothers might have been in the gallery.

A resolution of appreciation for the Senator's forty-two years of public service was passed unanimously. Another resolution urging him to continue his service to Virginia in the United States Senate was adopted by an overwhelming majority in a standing vote.

Byrd's change of mind, just two weeks after his first announcement, was addressed by way of reply to the General Assembly. The tribute and the clamor—together probably with certain political considerations—had led him "to accede to requests that I should be a candidate for re-election."

The incident is pertinent to the story of massive resistance and its fall, because that is above all a story of the mental processes and the political fortunes of Harry Byrd and Lindsay Almond. Byrd and his political organization had reached their lowest ebb in the gubernatorial election of 1953, when their candidate for governor barely scraped through to election.

The machine was now riding on the crest of the wave of defiance of the desegregation ruling.

Byrd, the architect of massive resistance, was at the peak of his prestige. Before many months had passed, the responsibility, and the onus and the anguish of soul, of meeting the commitments of that policy were to fall upon Lindsay Almond.

10. THE NAACP

THE National Association for the Advancement of Colored People thrived in Virginia. Its membership here, reaching 27,000 in 1958, was larger than in any other state in the South. No doubt because of the leadership taken by Senator Byrd and the state administration in the massive resistance movement, and of the relatively fragile popular base for such an extreme position in this state, the NAACP focused its greatest legal effort on Virginia. More school suits were filed here than in any other Southern state.

The thirteen Negro lawyers composing the legal staff of the Virginia Conference of the NAACP were headed by Oliver Hill, a lawyer of exceptional ability and a personally respected public figure. Hill had served one term on the Richmond City Council. Advising and reinforcing the Virginia group was the NAACP Legal Defense and Educational Fund, Inc., headed by the redoubtable Thurgood Marshall, who was himself a frequent visitor to this state. The regional counsel, one of the

four permanent representatives of the NAACP Legal Defense
and Educational Fund outside of New York, was a Negro
Virginian, Spotswood Robinson, of Richmond.

As a result of the intimidating effect of the "anti-NAACP"
laws enacted in September, 1956, NAACP membership in
Virginia had fallen off by about one-third, when on January
21, 1958, the most objectionable of these laws received a mortal
blow. On a suit for an injunction restraining enforcement of
five of the laws, a three-judge federal court declared three of
them unconstitutional. Two of the invalidated acts required
the registration of persons promoting legal or legislative action "on behalf of any race or color," or "whose activities tend
to cause racial conflicts or violence;" the third made it a crime
for a corporation such as the NAACP to "pay in whole or in
part" the expenses of any litigation in which it had only a
philanthropic interest. The court took a dim view of the other
two laws, but said that, since they were "vague and ambiguous,
we do not pass upon their constitutionality."

Hearing the case were Circuit Judge Morris A. Soper and
District Judges Walter E. Hoffman and Sterling Hutcheson.
Judge Hutcheson dissented, holding that the laws should have
been passed upon in the first instance by state courts.

The opinion which Judges Soper and Hoffman signed filled
forty legal-size typewritten pages. In addition to a review of
the legislative background of the laws under attack, citation of
precedents, etc., and extensive legal exposition, the opinion reflected a comprehensive study of the history, plan of organization, financial structure and activities of the NAACP. I propose to quote from that interesting document at some length.

It is difficult to describe the intensity with which the
NAACP was hated by white Virginians. Many who were
classed as moderates on the school issue hated the NAACP.
Fantastic rumors regarding the organization were given wide

credence. It was believed to be overflowing with money from
some sinister source. Its lawyers were believed to be working
for high financial rewards or, in some unexplained way, for
"political gain." Thousands of ignorant whites regarded the
NAACP as a Communist, or Communist-infiltrated, agency.
From better informed Virginians the Communist smear was
not heard as often as it is in the Deep South. Too many
NAACP leaders were well-known citizens of their communities. But even in these quarters the NAACP was regarded by
many as something diabolical.

It is appropriate to give the actual picture of the National
Association for the Advancement of Colored People in this
clear language of a federal court:

The activities of the Association cover 44 states, the District of
Columbia and the Territory of Alaska. It is the most important
Negro rights organization in the country . . . , having approximately 1,000 unincorporated branches. A branch consists of a group
of persons in a local community who enroll the minimum number
of members and, upon formal application to the main body, are
granted a charter. In Virginia, there are 89 active branches. A person becomes a member of a branch upon payment of dues which
amount, at a minimum, to $2.00 a year and may be more, at the
option of members, up to $500.00 for life membership. . . .

The principal source of income of the Association and its
branches consists of the membership fees which are solicited in
local membership drives. Other income is derived from special
fund-raising campaigns and individual contributions. In the first
eight months of the year the greater number of annual membership drives are conducted. During that period in 1957 the Association enrolled 13,595 members in Virginia. This represents a sharp
reversal in the rising trend in membership figures in the same eight-
month period in the preceding three years, which showed 13,583
members in 1954, 16,130 in 1955 and 19,436 in 1956. The income of
the Association from its Virginia branches during the first eight
months of 1957 was $37,470.60 as compared with $43,612.75 for the
same period in 1956. . . . The total income of the Association from

the country as a whole for the year 1956 was $598,612.84 and $425,-
608.13 for the first eight months of 1957.

At the top of the organizational structure of the national body
is the annual convention, which consists of delegates representing
the 1,000 branches in the several states. It has the power to establish policies and programs for the ensuing year which are binding
upon the Board of Directors and upon the branches of the Association. Each year the convention chooses sixteen members of a Board
of 48 Directors, each of whom serves for a term of three years. The
Board of Directors meets eleven times a year to carry out the
policies laid down by the convention. Under the Board an administrative staff is set up, headed by an executive secretary who,
representing the Board, presides over the functioning of the local
branches and state conferences throughout the country. . . .

The Virginia state conference takes the lead of the Association's
activities in the state under the administration of a full-time salaried
executive secretary, by whom the activities of the branches in the
state are coordinated and local membership and fund-raising campaigns are supervised. . . . Through its representatives, the state
conference appears before the General Assembly of Virginia and
state commissions in support of, or in opposition to, measures
which in its view advance or retard the status of the Negro in
Virginia. It encourages Negroes to comply with the statutes of the
state so as to qualify themselves to vote, and it conducts educational programs to acquaint the people of the state with the facts
regarding racial segregation and discrimination, and to inform Negroes as to their legal rights and to encourage the assertion of those
rights when they are denied. . . .

One of the most important activities of the state conference,
perhaps its most important activity, is the contribution it makes
to the prosecution of law suits brought by Negroes to secure their
constitutional rights. It has been found, through years of experience, that litigation is the most effective means to this end, when
Negroes are subjected to racial discrimination either by private
persons or by public authority. Accordingly, the Virginia state
conference maintains a legal committee, or legal staff, composed of
thirteen colored lawyers, located in seven communities scattered
over the greater part of the state. The members of the legal staff
are elected at the annual convention of the state conference, and

they in turn elect a chairman. Ordinarily the legal staff is called into action upon a complaint made to one or more members of the staff by aggrieved parties, but sometimes a grievance is brought directly to the attention of the executive secretary of the conference, and, if in his judgment the case presents a genuine grievance, involving discrimination on account of race or color, which falls within the scope of the work of the Association, he refers the parties to the legal staff. If the chairman approves the complaint, he recommends favorable action to the president of the conference and, if he concurs, the conference obligates itself to defray in whole or in part the costs and expenses of the litigation. With rare exceptions the attorneys selected by the complainant to bring the suit have been members of the legal staff. When a law suit has been completed, the attorney is compensated by the conference for out-of-pocket expenditures, including travel and stenographic services, and is also paid per diem compensation for the time spent in his professional capacity. No money ever passes directly to the plaintiff or litigant. The attorneys appear in the course of the litigation for and on behalf of the individual litigants, who in every instance authorize the institution of the suit.

. . . The fees paid the lawyers are modest in size and less than they would ordinarily earn for the time consumed.

The opinion also described the NAACP Legal Defense and Educational Fund, Inc., the separate national organization which cooperates with the Association in litigation on behalf of Negro citizens, of which the famous Thurgood Marshall is the chief counsel.

The Fund [the opinion notes] is governed by a Board of Directors which, under its charter, consists of not less than five and not more than fifty members. Its work is directed by the usual executive officers. It operates from an office in New York City and has no subordinate units. It employs a full time staff of six resident attorneys and three research attorneys stationed in New York City, and it keeps four lawyers on annual retainers in Richmond, Dallas, Los Angeles and Washington. It also engages local attorneys for investigation and research in particular cases. It has on call 100 lawyers throughout the country and a large number of social scientists who operate on a voluntary basis and work without pay or upon the payment of expenses only. . . .

The revenues of the Fund are derived solely from contributions received in response to letters sent out four times a year throughout the country by the Committee of One Hundred and, to some extent, from solicitations at small luncheons or dinners. There are no membership dues. . . . The income for 1956 was $351,283.32. . . .

The court's description of the embarrassment of the NAACP and of outspoken liberals of both races was an illuminating commentary on the emotional atmosphere in Virginia at this stage. After reviewing the series of steps in the massive resistance program, the opinion said:

It was in this setting that the acts now before the court were passed as parts of the general plan of massive resistance to the integration of schools of the state under the Supreme Court's decrees. The agitation involved in the widespread discussion of the subject, and the passage of the statutes by the Legislature, have had a marked effect upon the public mind, which has been reflected in hostility to the activities of the plaintiffs in these cases. This has been shown not only by the falling off of revenues, indicated above, but also by manifestations of ill will toward white and colored citizens who are known to be sympathetic with the aspirations of the colored people for equal treatment, particularly in the field of public education. A number of white people who attempted to give aid to the movement by speaking out on behalf of the colored people, or by taking membership in the Association, or joining the complainants in school suits, have been subjected to various kinds of annoyance. When their names appeared in the public press in connection with these activities, they were besieged day and night by telephone calls which were obscene, threatening, abusive, or merely silent interruptions to the peace and comfort of their homes. Letters and telegrams of like nature were also received. Some of these persons found themselves cut by their friends and made unwelcome where they had formerly been received with kindness and respect. Two crosses were burned near the homes of two of them; an effigy was hung in the yard of a white plaintiff in a school case, and a hearse was sent to the home of the colored president of the Norfolk branch of the Association during his absence "to pick up his body."

The court warned further with reference to the situation in Virginia that "the attitude of the public authorities openly encourages opposition to the law of the land, which may easily find expression in disturbances of the public peace."

Nevertheless, it is pertinent to record here the arresting phenomenon that through all the agitation and excitement of massive resistance in Virginia not a single instance of physical violence was reported.

11. SEGREGATION V. PUBLIC SCHOOLS

ACTUALLY, the expression, "massive resistance," was accurate now only with reference to a state of mind. Closing public schools, as far as it went, would end public school segregation, which the Supreme Court had ordered; it would not be in a strict sense resistance to the Court's rulings.

The idea of rebellion, or secession from the Union, was everywhere rejected. Governor Almond said in answer to a reporter's question: "That issue, sir, was resolved forever in the late War Between the States."

But closing schools would amount to resistance insofar as it would prevent a mingling of the races in open public schools, which was implicit in the Supreme Court's rulings. Above all, a sacrifice of public education, extremists believed, would show to the world the depth of Virginia's resentment of the Supreme Court's "intrusion."

What the ultimate result would be few attempted to predict. At the beginning Byrd may have hoped that, before the phalanx of massive resistance, federal courts in Virginia would temporize or evade their responsibilities. Any such fantasy was exploded when, on July 12, 1956, Federal District Judge John Paul—who, by the way, was a native Virginian and the son of a Confederate soldier—declared: "I am not willing that this court be a knowing and willing accessory to a policy which has as its purpose delay and evasion. . . ."—and ordered desegregation of Charlottesville's schools.

Byrd frequently held out the hope that the Supreme Court would "reverse its decision." Almond also had once said: "I have faith that the decision ultimately will be reversed." But this would not appear to have been a firm belief on the part of the Governor, and the prediction was rarely made in any other quarter.

Virginia lived for the moment, and for the moment massive resistance offered an exhilarating emotional outlet.

Meanwhile five Virginia desegregation suits ground slowly through the mill of argument, hearing, decision, appeal, and argument, hearing, etc., all over again. But by the summer of 1958 the period of possible delay was clearly drawing to an end. The seven-year-old case of Prince Edward County was approaching a climax, and Charlottesville, Norfolk and Arlington County seemed likely to face unappealable orders to begin desegregation in September. The Newport News case moved more slowly.

In July steps were taken leading to litigation in two more Virginia school districts. Six Negro pupils applied for the first time for admission to white schools in Richmond; and in a surprise move the Warren County school board received a request that it transfer twenty-five Negro pupils to the white high school and five Negro pupils to the white elementary school at the county seat of Front Royal. Warren, a county of 15,000 population, including approximately 1,200 Negroes, was one of seventeen Virginia counties which had no Negro high school. Its Negro high school pupils were sent to schools in two neighboring counties.

Yet in spite of all the agitation, relatively few Virginians in the summer of 1958 grasped the fact that massive resistance would actually boil down to locking the doors of public schools. The first to view this prospect realistically were the elements most earnestly concerned with the problem from the opposite extremes of the controversy. They were, on the one hand, the Defenders of State Sovereignty and, on the other, the Human Relations Councils and an incipient movement of opponents of massive resistance with the slogan: "Preserve the Public Schools."

The Defenders of State Sovereignty had taken steps as early as May 3 to form a "Co-ordinating Committee to Maintain Efficient Education in Virginia." ("Efficient education" here meant, not public education, but segregated private schools.) The organization was eventually to open an office in Richmond and take the name of the Virginia Education Fund. Its chairman from the start was Lewis S. Pendleton, a thirty-eight-year-old Richmond attorney and Defenders leader. Its object was to plan for, encourage and aid in the development of private schools to take the place of integrated public schools. It began to solicit funds; and it was in due course to make certain contributions to private school undertakings in Warren County, Charlottesville and Norfolk.

The *Richmond News Leader* gave enthusiastic endorsement to the private school movement and called for donations to its fund. That paper declared on June 6 that school-closing in some Virginia localities in September was "one of the few reasonable certainties in a most uncertain situation." It urged

private school promoters to get on with the "problems of housing, of teaching staff, of textbooks, of transportation, of tuition fees, of curriculum."

However, it is indicative of the lack of serious support in
the state as a whole for the idea of substituting private schools
for desegregated public schools that the Virginia Education
Fund never reached impressive proportions in members, funds
or prestige.

In Arlington County the Defenders attempted to establish a
small private school in a vacant residence, which failed to meet
the requirements of several county ordinances. The project met
with considerable ridicule also for a misspelled word in its sign,
"Grammer School." This initiative was soon abandoned. But
Charlottesville and Norfolk segregationists began to organize
private educational institutions which, on a reduced scale,
were to become more or less permanent.

Arlington County at that time was expected to be the first
district in which the school-closing laws would be brought
into play. Its school board was already under what seemed to
be peremptory federal court orders to admit Negro pupils to
white schools in September. As it happened, Arlington schools
were permitted to remain temporarily segregated for the first
semester. It thus escaped the impact of the massive resistance
laws, and no public schools ever closed in that county.

But Arlington County, on the outskirts of Washington, D. C.,
is often out of tune with Virginia policy and was particularly
so on the segregation issue. Its people, a cosmopolitan group
of relatively high average income, of whom only about 5 per
cent were Negroes, had little patience with the school-closing
legislation. Out of Arlington's present danger and the initiative
of its moderate citizens came a movement which was ultimately to reactivate thousands of Virginia moderates. The
movement's platform was contained in these declarations,

issued on May 1 by the organizing group of what was called the Arlington Committee to Preserve Public Schools:

1. We are determined to pursue every legal means to keep public schools open.
2. We are here concerned neither with perpetuating segregation in schools nor hastening integration.
3. We have faith in Arlington's ability to meet its public education problems.

By taking no position on the question of segregation, but concentrating entirely on the maintenance of public schools, the Arlington Committee to Preserve Public Schools quickly won the support of three elements: those who were openly in favor of desegregation, those who did not oppose desegregation but would shun any organization advocating it, and segregationists who were not so attached to segregation as to be willing to sacrifice public schools.

The Arlington Committee quickly drew public support. A meeting on June 12, at which its formal organization was completed, was attended by approximately 700 people. By the end of the month twenty-six of the thirty-nine white Parent-Teacher Associations in the county were on record in support of its activities, along with the Arlington Council of Churches, the League of Women Voters, the Council of Church Women and the local daily newspaper, the *Northern Virginia Sun*. The Arlington County governing board adopted a resolution urging the Governor to give his most earnest consideration to the views of the county's Committee to Preserve Public Schools. By the end of the summer the organization numbered over 3,000 members.

Meanwhile the Committee's representatives importuned Governor Almond; and its legal committee studied the possibility of court action to enjoin him from closing Arlington schools. It was decided that litigation would be deferred until after school-closing should become a fact. Had any Arlington school actually been closed, not only would legal action have been promptly instituted to require its reopening, but organized protest would have taken place on a large scale. '

As the summer of 1958 wore on, with the usual resort to mountains, seashore and local fishing haunts, there was an ominous silence on the subject of the desegregation crisis in most of Virginia. Colgate Darden, president of the University of Virginia, who had broken with his former associates of the Byrd organization over massive resistance, declared that to close public schools "would be an irreparable blow." But Darden saw no possibility of arresting the trend at this juncture. The attitude of most moderate leaders—and they included a number who had played a distinguished part in the affairs of the commonwealth—is best summed up in the remark made to me by one of them:

There's nothing you or I can do at this stage. We would only be denounced as "integrationists." Some schools will have to close. Sad as it is, it will take the actual fact of closed schools to restore sanity in this state. Virginia is going to have to learn the hard way.

12. PRINCE EDWARD AGAIN

IN THE final weeks before the September school opening, attention focused on Arlington, Charlottesville and Norfolk, and to a less extent upon the relatively new case of Warren County, where Negroes had not applied for admission to the white high school until July 18. On August 4, Prince Edward

County was once more removed from the critical list by a decision handed down by Federal District Judge Sterling Hutcheson.

It had been the lot of this quiet, thoughtful, kindly jurist, himself a Southside Virginian, to deal with the supremely difficult Prince Edward County case almost continuously since the 1954 Supreme Court decision. A humanitarian, Judge Hutcheson was noted for his courteous attention to the pleading of all manner of defendants as well as for his scrupulous firmness in applying the law. His personal views on race segregation were not definitely known even to his friends; he never discussed the issue out of court. But he was born in Mecklenburg County and he maintained a home in Brunswick, two neighboring counties each with a heavier Negro population than Prince Edward. Sterling Hutcheson was steeped in Southern tradition; he was also preeminently a man of conscience.

In each hearing on Prince Edward the NAACP attorneys urged school desegregation at the beginning of the next following school term. Judge Hutcheson declared that "the law has been announced by the Supreme Court and must be observed," but he strove to educe the last modicum of indulgence from the high court's language and to put off issuing an order the immediate effects of which would be patently disastrous.

In a decision of January 23, 1957, he had traced the history of Prince Edward County and its race problem from the settlement of the county in the middle of the eighteenth century to the present, and said with reference to the existing situation:

Buttressed by popular demand of the people of the county since the decision in the first Brown case, evidenced in part by a petition signed by more than 4,000 residents, the board of supervisors has declined to allocate funds for the operation of schools on an annual basis. Instead, it appropriates the necessary operating expenses on a monthly basis, with a publicly declared intention of discontinuing that appropriation if schools in the county are mixed racially at this time.

The Judge concluded that "at this time a continuation of present methods could not be so harmful [to the colored children] as an interrupted education." He had declined to order desegregation within any fixed period of time.

"I believe the problems to be capable of solution," Judge Hutcheson said, "but they will require patience, time and a sympathetic understanding. . . ."

Many people, including, to my knowledge, many Negroes, would have been happy to see the "impossible" Prince Edward County case left with that admirable observation of this federal district judge. But the NAACP attorneys noted appeal. On November 11, 1957, the United States Fourth Circuit Court returned the case to Judge Hutcheson with the instruction: "We think that the district judge was in error in not fixing a time limit for compliance."

The petition mentioned by Judge Hutcheson had indeed been signed by 4,216 Prince Edward residents over twenty-one years of age. That was about 1,000 more than the total number of qualified voters in the county. The petition said in part:

We, the undersigned citizens of Prince Edward County, Virginia, . . . do affirm that we prefer to abandon public schools and educate our children in some other way if that be necessary to preserve separation of the races in the schools of this county. . . .

The white private school organization stood ready to move into action, but no schooling of any kind was in prospect for the Negro children of Prince Edward if the public schools should be closed.

Another soul-searching ordeal confronted the gentle Southside Virginia jurist. Again he recoiled from precipitating inevitable distress. In his new opinion, delivered on August 4, Judge Hutcheson indulged in these philosophical reflections:

We hear such terms as "the jet age," a "new day" and "crash programs" used as excuses for speedy action. These catch phrases are not consistent with the "deliberate speed," the "unhurrying chase," ascribed by Thompson to his "Hound of Heaven." Furthermore, they are not applicable to the situation with which we are dealing. Despite the great advances in scientific and technical knowledge we have no evidence on which to base a belief that in accepting new theories of social or moral reform the modern human mind is any more adaptable than that of the Athenian of 500 B.C. The knowledge of preceding generations can be preserved in writings but wisdom cannot be transmitted by inheritance. It must be acquired by experience. . . .

We find that following the adoption of his code of laws, Solon, in order to afford a period for its acceptance by the people and to avoid importunities for interpretation, modification, etc., absented himself for ten years during which he visited foreign countries. Upon his return there yet remained much to be done.

With the example of Solon apparently in mind, Judge Hutcheson fixed the first school opening ten years from the Supreme Court ruling of May, 1955, as the tentative deadline for the desegregation of Prince Edward County's public schools. As a gesture of legal defense the county's school board had undertaken to engage a consultant to assist in a survey of its school desegregation problem. The board was ordered to report the following January on the qualifications of its consultant and the progress made by that date. The court also noted that the 1965 deadline would be subject to modifications, including specifically a modification "accelerating or extending the date of compliance. . . ."

Although the opinion was far from the massive resistance thesis, it was applauded in massive resistance circles. Governor Almond recommended that every Virginia community facing the school desegregation problem should undertake a survey of the type contemplated in Prince Edward County, and said:

"I commend to all concerned in positions of authority as well as to all the people of Virginia this constructive approach to the beginning of a solution of a grave problem fraught with every potential of crisis and disaster."

But, though they delayed acting until the following December, the attorneys of the National Association for the Advancement of Colored People were to appeal the case once more.

13. THE APPROACH OF ZERO HOUR

No OFFICIAL body in Virginia strove as long or as courageously as Chairman Paul Schweitzer and the school board of Norfolk to bring about a lawful and orderly solution of the school desegregation problem. As early as June, 1955, Norfolk's superintendent of schools, who was eventually to preside with conspicuous success over the first school integration in that city, had declared publicly that Norfolk schools could be desegregated without great difficulty; a few days later the school board—which was soon to be hamstrung by state policy—had announced:

"We intend, without mental reservation, to uphold and abide by the law of the land."

On the other hand, no city officials were more stubbornly set upon resistance or more hostile to any constructive move than Mayor W. Fred Duckworth and members of the Norfolk city council. Apart from the conflicting concern of these two bodies and in spite of the almost constant and much publicized litigation over Norfolk's schools, the attitude of the populace of this, Virginia's largest city, was one of phenomenal apathy.

Election records show a high percentage of liberal voters in Norfolk (27 per cent of whose population is Negro). There were other evidences of a large, though unorganized, moderate element in that city's relatively cosmopolitan population. Meetings had been held looking toward the organization of a Norfolk Committee for Public Schools. But only a small number had been alerted to the gravity of the approaching crisis. Moderate leadership also, in Norfolk as elsewhere, was largely cowed by the abusive tactics of extreme segregationists; the Norfolk branch of the Defenders of State Sovereignty was particularly aggressive.

As the date for the 1958 school opening approached, the situation in Norfolk was marked not only by indifference on the part of many, but by confusion and unreadiness on the part of the divergent groups who were alive to the possibility that some of that city's schools would indeed not open. In spite of extravagant assurances from the promoters of the segregationist Tidewater Educational Foundation, Norfolk was the least prepared of the affected localities to accommodate displaced public school pupils in private schools. Although the school board, under federal court order, had approved the applications of seventeen Negro students for admission to white schools, most of the city's over 275,000 residents believed until the last moment that a crisis would be averted somehow by a retreat either by the court or by the state.

In Arlington County, on the other hand, a formidable Committee for Public Schools, backed by overwhelming public sentiment, stood poised for swift action in the event desegregation, which had been ordered by the court, should result in the closing of any school in that county.

In Warren County, where a desegregation suit was filed only on August 29, most citizens assumed that no serious trouble need be anticipated at least for many months to come.

If any community was earnestly concerned over the situation from all angles, it was Charlottesville, the city of Jefferson and the University of Virginia. This was the first locality after the original case of Prince Edward County to receive desegregation orders from a federal court. During the litigation and sundry delays since the original ruling in August, 1956, its 27,000 citizens had had little opportunity to get the problem out of mind. Having among them an unusual proportion of extremists as well as intellectuals, they had experienced more agitation on both sides of the desegregation issue than any other Virginia community.

Charlottesville's Negro population (18.2 per cent of the total) was exceptionally progressive and alert; the Charlottesville unit of the NAACP had won the first award in a national membership contest. The Charlottesville Council on Human Relations was one of the largest and most active of those desegregationist organizations in the state. A Charlottesville Committee to Preserve Public Schools was in process of formation.

On the other side of the argument Charlottesville had one of the most active chapters of the Defenders of State Sovereignty, and it had had for a time a White Citizens Council. Plans for segregationist private schools were well advanced. Charlottesville had been visited by such well-known itinerant agitators as John Kasper and Asa Carter. Segregationist mass meetings had rallied 1,000 or more people. Segregationist petitions had been presented and leaflets left at nearly every door. Crosses had been burned in four instances near the meeting place of the Council on Human Relations or at the homes of persons active in it. Feeling ran high on both sides of the controversy.

Through it all Charlottesville had been blessed with a

firmly constructive city administration and a discreetly moderate school board. It is significant also that in the Democratic primary of the previous April, Robert R. Ready, a bitter-end resister and advocate of segregation at all costs, had campaigned strenuously for a seat on the city council and had been badly beaten.

The Charlottesville mayor is elected by the city council from among its members. Chosen for the next term was an able leader, who played a distinguished role throughout the desegregation unrest in that city. In taking office on September 1, Mayor Thomas J. Michie delivered to the council, and through the press to the people of Charlottesville, a brief address which at the time and place required rare courage. The new mayor said in part:

> Our immediate problem is, of course, the school question. We do not know just what course events in the next few weeks or months —or even years—may take. But I do know this—I know that every member of the School Board will be guided in whatever actions we take by these principles: Respect for our Courts and their orders, a determination to preserve law and order in this City at any cost and a determination to do everything in our power to preserve our public school system.

> I know that we shall all be guided by those principles in what we do. But, being guided by those principles, we may therefore be compelled to take action which will be distasteful to every member of this Council and of the School Board, distasteful to the overwhelming majority of those of our citizens who may be most affected by it—and actually abhorrent to many who feel most strongly about it.

> If this should be the case, I must urge our citizens to remain calm and to accept what may be forced upon us as good citizens should. There may be some, quite possibly agitators from other areas, who will argue that our citizens should take matters in their own hands and try by physical violence to prevent obedience to the orders of the courts. I have enough confidence in the good sense of our people to feel sure that no such effort will actually be

made here. But I must warn those agitators who may endeavor to make trouble that violence and mob action will not be tolerated here. . . . Our police force is on the alert. It is loyal and efficient and it will tolerate no disorder and no efforts to provoke disorder.

For thirty-six years it had been the custom of Senator Byrd to hold a mass picnic every Labor Day week-end, to which he invited friends, fellow apple-orchardists and, as the years went by, an ever-increasing number of politicians. Byrd's 1958 picnic, held on August 30, drew a record-breaking crowd. Box lunches were served to some 3,800 in his Berryville orchards. It was a bright, sunshiny Saturday. Byrd, clad in a double-breasted white suit, light blue shirt and red tie, roamed over the sloping lawn, greeting guests and exchanging both apple and political lore.

After the lunches of fried chicken and ham, the crowd clustered around a speaking platform and heard the Senator, now in shirt-sleeves, discuss Virginia's "greatest crisis since the war between the states."

"We Virginians seek only to preserve our school system," Byrd said, "the right to run it, and to preserve the sovereignty of our Commonwealth which is our most sacred heritage. This is the objective of our massive resistance to the Warren court decision. . . ."

Of the NAACP he said: "They want to bring Virginia to its knees first and then, after conquering Virginia—though I think they will have a little trouble doing it—they intend to march through the South singing hallelujah."

Asked specifically by reporters what steps he thought the state should take if and when some integrated school enrollment might be achieved, Byrd said that Almond was in charge of state school policy and he stood "firmly and four-square" behind the Governor.

Speaker of the House Blackburn Moore presented to the

Senator a framed scroll carrying the General Assembly's lauda-
tory resolution of the previous February, signed by all 100 of
the House members and thirty-one of the forty state senators.
Byrd was also handed a letter in which Governor Almond, who
was unable to be present, hailed him as "the greatest living
American."

The next day Byrd and Moore, his hiking companion of old,
took off for a ten-day visit to Alaska.

In Richmond, Lindsay Almond walked on toward the gathering storm, into the conflicting pressures and the anxious inquiries of school officials, into the barrage of questions from
press and radio and the dubious glare of national publicity, and
into the climax of his own inner struggle—strangely alone.

14. LIGHTNING STRIKES WARREN

FEW spots in Virginia had seemed farther removed from the
school segregation controversy than little, mountain-locked
Warren County, in the northern corner of the state. Most of
Warren's white citizens had paid scant attention to the segregation furor; and, with only a handful of Negro residents in
their midst, they were not conscious of any race problem
affecting them.

True, not all of the county's Negro school children were
adequately provided for. Warren was one of the seventeen
Virginia counties which had no Negro high school. But money
had been appropriated for a new consolidated elementary and
secondary school to be erected within a year, and in the meantime its 106 Negro high school pupils presumably would con-

tinue to be sent to high schools in neighboring counties. Though the latter arrangement involved certain hardships and an inferior educational offering, it was expensive for the tax-payers and was regarded by many as a kind of largesse on be-half of the county's Negro children.

Twenty-two of the Negro high school students had per-sisted in their applications for admission to the white high school at the county seat of Front Royal. Their applications being rejected, their attorneys had filed suit on August 29. On September 8, the Warren County school board received an order from Federal District Judge John Paul restraining it from refusing admission to the twenty-two applicants. On the following Thursday, September 11, Judge Simon E. Sobeloff of the Fourth Circuit Court of Appeals denied a stay of the order. A day later Warren County High School became the first school to close under Virginia's massive resistance laws.

Governor Almond addressed the following notice to Q. D. Gasque, the Warren County Superintendent of Schools:

Under compulsion of an order issued by the U. S. District Court for the Western District of Virginia, both white and colored chil-dren have been enrolled effective September 15, 1958, in the War-ren County High School, located in the county of Warren.

Pursuant to the provisions of Chapter 9.1 of the Code of Virginia, the Warren County High School is closed and is removed from the public school system, effective September 15, 1958, and all authority, power and control over such school, its principal, teach-ers, other employees and all pupils now enrolled or ordered to be enrolled, will thereupon be vested in the Commonwealth of Vir-ginia, to be exercised by the governor.

Accordingly, by virtue of the authority vested in me as chief executive of the Commonwealth of Virginia, I will thereupon as-sume all power and control over such school and hereby request all local officials and all citizens to cooperate with the Department of State Police and local law enforcement officers in the protection of public property and the security of public peace and order.

You are requested to forthwith notify all teachers and other personnel connected with such school, and all parents and other persons having the custody and care of all pupils enrolled or ordered to be enrolled in such school, of this action.

(Almost simultaneously that evening of September 12, 1958, Governor Orval Faubus issued his order closing the senior high schools of Little Rock, Arkansas.)

Warren's travail was later to become a *cause célèbre*. The little county was to be visited and indoctrinated by segregationists from far and near. It was to be torn with bitter dissension, not so much involving its Negro citizens as among white people, businessmen, organized labor, social and church groups. For a short time in 1959, "Warren County" would be a symbol throughout the South less familiar only than "Little Rock."

But in mid-September, 1958, the structure of common sense and good will in Warren was still intact. A *Richmond Times-Dispatch* report from the area on the day after the high school was officially closed read in part as follows:

Public opinion here Monday seemed to grow in favor of integrating the shut-down Warren County High School, while state officials possibly considered an attempt to reorganize it on a segregated basis.

. . . Local officials acknowledged they were confused. Most residents are perplexed and say they don't know what will come next.

One possible way of reorganizing the school would be to persuade the twenty-two Negro applicants to withdraw their application for enrollment. That possibility is highly unlikely, officials here believe.

"Our hands are pretty well tied," E.T. Shiner, chairman of the Warren County school board said Monday. "Our people haven't caught their breath yet."

Superintendent Gasque told reporters: "I am constrained to believe that this town could work out its own solution."

The chairman of the county board of supervisors, E. Maurice

Bowers, said: "I think the people would prefer segregation, but they'd rather have integration than closed schools."

County Judge W. Leroy Corren said he believes a local option plan is the "only way out" for Virginia. "We don't have any Little Rock here," the judge said.

The article reported no local comment in approval of the closing of the school.

In my column in the *Washington Post* I addressed an open letter to the people of Warren County. It had doubtless little effect, but because of its commentary on the psychological and the legal situations, and its forecast, it may be appropriate to quote the following from it here:

The desegregation crisis has come rather suddenly to your beautiful and peaceful county. Until a few weeks ago, many of you had not followed its developments closely or given the matter much attention. It seemed like something far away.

Now you have met it head-on. Your high school is closed. You are uncertain and apprehensive, though to your great credit you are not excited. I hope you will remain calm right through to the end of this trouble.

From a wide observation of the problem, I would say that calmness is the key to it. Try to fill the prolonged vacation of the high school students with healthy, preferably educational, activities—there is work for civic leaders there—and go on about your business. Go on about the business of building a better county, and a better town of Front Royal, which has such a bright future.

At the same time, the school problem needs to be quietly studied, and quietly a solution will be found. Begin by sweeping out trashy rumors. This trouble wasn't stirred up by the Communists, any more than by the Purple People-Eaters. It is a step in the implementation of a decision of the Supreme Court of the United States.

Warren County High School was not closed by the Negroes who asked for integration. That has happened in hundreds of other places, and it doesn't close any school. Your high school was closed by the Governor of Virginia, who acted in accordance with legislation enacted by the General Assembly. That legislation is impracticable and probably unconstitutional as well. The state administration itself has instituted proceedings to test its validity. It will not remain in effect very long, you may be sure.

Even under that legislation, if your board of supervisors and your School Board request it, the Governor may release your high school and let you open it again. I am sure you want him to do that. Consequently, citizens should write to Governor Almond in Richmond, telling him that you want your school reopened. Or you should form an organization to insist on this.

Warren County will lose some money, temporarily, when the school is reopened this way, but nothing is more certain than that the law for cutting off state funds will be invalidated or repealed in the not very distant future.

15. MASSIVE RESISTANCE GOES ALL THE WAY

THE FIRST school-closing under massive resistance fell upon Virginia complacency with a heavy thud.

Warren County had been seldom heard from in the past; the very name had been unfamiliar to many Virginians. Now, with the aid of daily newspaper stories and photographs and radio and television broadcasts, the state suddenly became aware both of Warren County and of the practical effect of the massive resistance legislation. At the same time, attention turned with new anxiety to the ripening crises in Arlington, Charlottesville and Norfolk. (In the existing legal situations it was evident that the Newport News and Richmond suits had still a long way to travel.) Alarmed citizens in Charlottesville and Norfolk began to canvass the available housing for private school classes.

There was little public comment on the course which the state was pursuing, no important challenge of the policy which was moving so fast toward disaster. But the *Richmond News Leader* sought to accelerate the movement to set up private schools to replace desegregated public schools. That paper said:

> There was some feeling, as the prospect of school-closing was discussed this summer, that "it can't happen here." Well it has happened in Warren County, and it will happen elsewhere, and it will do us no particular good to be "stunned" or "shocked" into a state of paralysis. . . .
>
> What we are faced with in Virginia right now, is the necessity of establishing a workable, well-financed, capably administered system of genuine private schools. . . . If we want our children educated in an atmosphere free of the evils of race-mixing, then we will have to do it ourselves. And wherever integration threatens, whether in Warren County or right here in Richmond, we had better set promptly about doing it.

Governor Almond took occasion to point out: "I have repeatedly stated that our position is not one of defiance. No federal court has the authority to compel any state to operate any schools. They may force us to the position where we must abandon public schools. . . . That is not defiance of federal authority."

Little Warren County, meanwhile, was aided, advised and harassed from all sides, while its confused citizens struggled to arrive at some clear course of action. For the first time, an earnest pro-public schools faction and a fiercely pro-massive resistance faction developed in the county, with the latter in the ascendancy. Frantic efforts were being made to form some kind of organization to provide private school classes for the county's white high school children.

The Warren County High School had opened on September 2 and operated through September 12, when the closing order came. School-opening was postponed in Arlington and repeatedly in Charlottesville and Norfolk, while officials and attorneys continued to engage in feverish efforts to stave off desegregation orders for those three cities.

In fact, Arlington, rather than Warren, had been the center of attention during the hot, sultry days of the first week of September. The Arlington school board and the State Pupil Placement Board had rejected the applications of thirty Negro children as unqualified for admission to the white schools in which they sought to be enrolled. For three days, lawyers and educators debated the criteria used and the qualifications of these Negro youngsters—much of the time with the latter sitting in the Alexandria courtroom. On September 8, Federal District Judge Albert V. Bryan gave his approval for the opening of Arlington schools on a segregated basis, while he weighed his decision on the Negro applications.

Judge Bryan concluded that four of the applications had been improperly rejected. On September 17, he ordered the four Negro children admitted to Arlington's Stratford Junior High School. But—to the vast relief of Governor Almond and the proponents of massive resistance—the federal judge said that, since the fall term had already started, he would not require compliance with the order until the beginning of the next term in February. A school-closing explosion of incalculable reverberations was thus averted in the one locality which was openly and overwhelmingly opposed to the state's school policy.

In Norfolk some extremists felt that the school board had yielded too easily to federal court pressure when it enrolled seventeen Negro pupils in white schools, even though the board was seeking court permission to postpone their actual admission another year. A special meeting of the Defenders of

State Sovereignty in Richmond, September 1, had called upon the Governor to "negate and reverse" this action, pointing out that the power to assign pupils was now vested in the State Pupil Placement Board. The school boards of both Norfolk and Charlottesville were also under injunctions from state courts, effective until October 15, restraining them from making any school assignments.

On September 4, Governor Almond had addressed a warning to the school authorities of four localities, Norfolk, Arlington, Charlottesville and Prince Edward, that "such an affirmative act of assignment would constitute a voluntary act on the part of the local board, bringing upon it the onus of creating the condition which would invoke the applicable statute, closing the schools."

The Governor's message was dispatched from Richmond with an unusual flourish. Uniformed state police took the letters from the Governor's hand and sped posthaste in state cars in various directions to deliver them to the addressees. (The gubernatorial courier with the missive for Arlington Superintendent Ray E. Reid located his addressee in the federal court in Alexandria, where he was attending a hearing on the Arlington case. The state trooper was required to leave his revolver outside and deliver the document to a federal court functionary!)

But in the Charlottesville and Norfolk cases the legal machinery ground inexorably on to peremptory desegregation orders, and the harsh implementation of massive resistance. On September 19 Governor Almond paraphrased his notice to the Warren County board, and closed two Charlottesville schools. They were Lane High School, with approximately 1,050 pupils, and Venable Elementary School, with approximately 650. Similarly, on September 27 Norfolk's six white high schools, with a total enrollment of approximately 10,000, were closed. About 1,000 pupils already had been locked out of the Warren County high school.

At the end of September, 12,700 Virginia children were out of their public schools. Approximately 2,000 of these had been hastily accommodated in private classes or tutoring groups. A few hundred had found refuge in public schools of other districts. The rest were waiting for somebody to do something to get them back in school.

No one shouted: "Hurrah!" And no loud voice cried: "For shame!" The initial reaction of most Virginians to these events was one of stunned silence.

This was it. This was what the politicians had been talking about. Thousands had never believed the politicians really meant what they said; here was a visual demonstration. Nine public schools had been closed. And this might be only the beginning; it might go on and on. Schools might be closed in district after district, as fast as Negro plaintiffs, NAACP lawyers and the courts should move.

But there was no immediate wave of protest. If they saw that this was a prohibitive price to pay for preventing gradual admission of Negro pupils to white schools, the fear of retaliation and abuse still gripped many citizens. It is stretching far, of course, to compare the odium which had been heaped upon advocates of compliance with the desegregation ruling with the treatment accorded the early Christians in Rome, but it is apt to observe that moderates in Virginia had fled to the catacombs of disinvolvement. It would take time for them to emerge.

16. RESORT TO PRIVATE SCHOOLS

THE PICTURE presented in some quarters of Virginia communities abandoning public education rather than accept integration was misleading with respect to the melancholy events of September, 1958. The closing of public schools in Warren County, Charlottesville and Norfolk was not an act of local initiative. No school administrator, no school board, no local authority voluntarily closed any school; and no Parent-Teacher Association, no group of school patrons asked that their school be closed. The schools were closed by the Governor of Virginia in pursuance of an act of the Virginia General Assembly.

As we have seen, the immediate reaction in Warren County was not one of satisfaction or approval. From Charlottesville a delegation presented to the Governor a petition, carrying the signatures of a majority of the pupils of Lane High School, asking that their school be allowed to re-open. Students at two of the closed schools in Norfolk mounted placards and signed petitions in favor of re-opening their schools. The P-TA of Norfolk's Norview High School voted sixty-five to sixty-four in favor of trying to get that school re-opened.

Aggressive opposition to re-opening the schools without complete segregation was to develop during coming weeks in each of the three localities; a majority of voters were to register their opposition to such a step in Norfolk in a November referendum. But it was not local resistance to desegregation which closed the schools in the first instance.

By the same token, the resort to private schools was not actually an escape from integrated public schools; it was an escape from no schools at all. Whatever the feeling about the

Supreme Court's rulings, or the state's package of laws to prevent integration—and many never clearly understood this complicated matter—12,700 pupils in Warren County, Charlottesville and Norfolk had been locked out of their public schools, and the most urgent concern of those communities was to get those children into some kind of school.

A few children whose parents could afford the expense were placed in regular private schools, but the few dozen vacancies in the regular private schools of Virginia were quickly filled. Displaced Virginia pupils were sent to schools in other states, some as far away as California and Connecticut. Ironically, some of these displaced pupils were accommodated in racially integrated schools in other states. A handful were also placed in public schools of other Virginia localities.

But the great majority of the displaced pupils were left without any opportunity for schooling except in such private schools and tutoring classes as might hastily be improvised. Parents, ministers, civic leaders and other public-spirited persons in each of the three localities addressed themselves strenuously to this challenge.

The resort to private schools thus was not entirely either an evasive maneuver or an effort to perpetuate segregation. Many promoters of private schools viewed them only as temporary expedients to be abandoned as soon as public schools should be reopened, even on an integrated basis. In several instances leaders of white tutoring groups indicated that Negroes would not be denied admission to them if they should apply.

The private school improvisations having assumed this character, the objection to making use of church property was largely removed. Many ministers cooperated with the movement and Sunday School rooms and other church premises were frequently used.

The best prepared of the three affected communities was

Charlottesville, where the pro-massive resistance Charlottes-ville Educational Foundation and the pro-public schools Parents' Committee for Emergency Schooling joined forces. In a temporary truce in the segregation quarrel, the education of children became the overriding objective, and public-spirited citizens rallied everywhere to meet the school challenge. Within a few weeks virtually all of the 1,700 displaced Charlottesville pupils were receiving some instruction.

In Norfolk more schools had closed and fewer preparations had been made. Until the last moment most Norfolkians had hoped that a showdown would be averted, or that the state would retreat, once it came to closing schools. Then the Tide-water Educational Foundation, which had announced its readiness to accommodate 4,500 children, almost failed to get its project off the ground. Its "Tidewater Academy" finally opened with less than 100 pupils. By mid-October, of Norfolk's 10,000 displaced pupils, only about 3,000 were enrolled in private tutoring groups; about 500 were enrolled in public schools of neighboring localities; and about 900 were attending night classes in the high school of South Norfolk (a separate city). Most parents still believed that, somehow or other, the schools would re-open within a few days.

A ruling from Federal District Judge John Paul that the operation of private segregated schools with publicly-paid teachers would be "in clear violation of the mandate of the United States Supreme Court" caused the newly-formed Warren County Educational Foundation to postpone until late in October the opening of its private classes; it had expected to use public school teachers in them. In Charlottesville, however, City Attorney John Battle, Jr., expressed the opinion that public school teachers might teach in the private school program until such time as that program might be shown to be discriminatory, and a number of public school teachers taught in the private schools there.

In Norfolk, the Tidewater Academy found its operations delayed and curtailed by its inability to obtain the services of public school teachers. The Academy being an undertaking of the bitterly segregationist Defenders of State Sovereignty, the teachers feared that teaching in it would identify them with massive resistance and involve them in embarrassing legal complications. Directors of the Foundation appeared before assembled teachers from the closed schools, explained their program, and asked the teachers to lend their services. Only one public school teacher agreed to serve.

However, Norfolk teachers, who had been made idle by school-closing, themselves took the lead in establishing what they called "tutoring groups." These classes, meeting frequently in Sunday School buildings, were set up with the understanding that they were strictly temporary, that they were only to fill the gap until the public schools should re-open.

In Warren County, by mid-October only 162 seniors out of the high school's approximately 1,000 pupils had been accommodated in the improvised private classes; but a drive to provide more ample private school facilities had raised $83,000 toward a $175,000 goal.

Negro schools remained open in all three of the affected localities. However, the Negroes ordered to be admitted to white schools refused to enroll in Negro schools for fear of impairing their legal standing. In Charlottesville and Norfolk these Negro children were accommodated in private tutoring classes. The twenty-two Negro children, plaintiffs in the Warren County case, attended public schools in Washington, D. C.; and a fund was raised by public subscription to meet their expenses.

17. THE THOUGHTS OF LINDSAY ALMOND

UNLIKE Senator Byrd, whose public statements on the desegregation problem were few and tersely consistent, Lindsay Almond uttered many thousands of words on the subject and voiced a variety of extravagant opinions.

As a lawyer for the Virginia defendants in the school cases, in the original litigation, Attorney General Almond had told the Supreme Court respectfully, "I have advised and will advise the officers of my state to proceed with all expedition to work out a solution." But in August, 1958, Governor Almond in a press conference said flatly: "The State of Virginia and the localities of Virginia cannot . . . and will not operate mixed schools."

Attorney General Almond said in a federal court in September, 1956:

In the first place, I think I may say to your honor with propriety that I believe I can say that, notwithstanding the remark of the counsel of the opposition, in every official deliverance that I have made on the subject, even my opinion on the so-called interposition resolution, which was not a popular position, but, I hope, correct, I recognize the binding effect and force of the decision of the Supreme Court of the United States.

Yet Governor Almond told reporters on November 5, 1958: "I do not recognize, I have never recognized, I cannot recognize that what the Supreme Court says is the law of the land."

Having warned the Supreme Court earlier that the desegregation problem could not be solved "with uniformity of approach at the state level," Almond fought fiercely for uniformity of approach at the state level. No one insisted more vehemently than he that a "little integration" in any section of Virginia would be impossible without sweeping integration everywhere, and that this would destroy the public school system.

Almond said: "Irrefutable evidence abundantly abounds that the mixing of races in our public schools will isolate them from the support of the public, produce strife, bitterness, chaos and confusion to the utter destruction of any rational concept of a public school system."

In one interview he said: "Violence would result. . . . We would live almost in a police state. . . . It would mean there would have to be police guards in and out and around the schools. . . ."

Yet, when public schools were desegregated in three Virginia localities five months later, the operation was carried out in an atmosphere of tranquillity and order unexcelled in any state.

It is not an inspiring exercise to seek out inconsistencies in the utterances of an active and sorely tried leader in a period of tension and agitation. What politician is qualified to cast the first stone? Almond's fire-and-brimstone oratory was a part of his stock in trade, but his easily generated anger was not all affected, and it sometimes got out of control. In the boundless inconsistencies into which political considerations or loss of temper or sheer verbosity may have led Lindsay Almond, there was one significant element of consistency: he insisted upon a hair-splitting distinction between federal "power" and federal "authority;" he never crossed the line of actual defiance of federal court orders. Almond placed a degree of emphasis upon the power of federal courts and the inevitability of ultimate compliance with their orders which was unusual among massive resistance leaders.

It should be recorded also that, though under pressure to do so on a number of occasions, Almond never lent himself to any

move of intimidation or reprisal with respect to Virginia's
Negro citizens.

One of the massive resistance laws included a provision that,
when a school should be closed on account of integration, the
governor should attempt to reassign pupils and "reorganize"
the school on a segregated basis. This was understood to mean
that the governor personally should visit the affected school
district and negotiate with the parents of Negro children seeking admission to white schools. Such a gesture, with its inevitable aura of power and circumstance, would have required
great courage on the part of the Negroes to resist.

This vague provision Almond completely ignored. Asked to
comment on some local efforts to induce Negro pupils to withdraw their applications for enrollment in Warren County High
School, the Governor told reporters that withdrawal of the
Negro pupils would naturally result in the re-opening of the
school, but he added emphatically that his statement was not
to be taken as "pressure or coercion" aimed at the Negroes
involved.

"My position is clear," Almond said. "I will not permit the
office of governor to be used to coerce or take undue advan-
tage of any citizen relative to that citizen's concept of his or
her constitutional rights. . . ."

When, in later stages of the massive resistance aberration,
the Norfolk city council took steps, out of pure spite, to force
the closing of that city's Negro high schools, the Governor
commented angrily that this "would be a vicious and retalia-
tory blow against the Negro race." For his part, Almond said:
"I would not want to be charged with harboring such a spirit."

Almond's press conference of September 16, 1958, following
the first school-closing, was one of his most revealing. Pressures and queries beat down on him now from every quarter.
His face was familiar to newspaper and magazine readers and

television viewers, across the nation. His name was widely coupled with that of Governor Faubus of Arkansas. Attended by twenty-two reporters, seven television cameras and several still photographers, this was the largest press conference he had ever held.

Asked for comment on the decision of the Norfolk school board, against his advice, to stand firm in its admission of seventeen Negro pupils to white schools, Almond said: "I recognize they stand under coercive power of the federal court. I would hesitate as a lawyer to advise my client to go to jail when I couldn't go with him!"

On the question of interposing the Governor's authority to take over and reopen Warren High School on a segregated basis, he said:

Neither this state nor any other state has the power successfully to interpose itself between a subject matter and the overriding power of the Federal Government.

I would be delighted to do that, [he added] . . . but there's a little difficulty in the offing. . . . That is, the state could be enjoined, the governor could be enjoined, his agents could be enjoined from operating in violation of the federal decrees. . . . You're getting back to interposition . . . and interposition does not have that efficacy.

Asked if he envisioned putting himself as governor in direct opposition to the power of the federal courts, he replied:

"Well, I haven't reached that stage. . . . If putting myself in such a position would do any good, I would be delighted to do so. . . . But I would not want to do a vain thing. . . . I would want to be fully advised before deciding."

Would he accept a federal court summons, if it came to that?

No citizen, whatever his capacity, is immune to a process issuing from a court of competent jurisdiction, from a state court or a

federal court. . . . I would certainly not want to be ugly about
it. . . . Any process to which I was legally amenable, I would not
undertake to impede. . . . It would not be in keeping with the
dignity of the office of governor. I would not want to assume an
attitude of defiance.

How did Almond feel? What did he think and what did he
hope? What did he see at the end of the road? What Almond's
innermost thoughts were in the fall of 1958 has been a subject
of unending speculation since. The question, no doubt, will
intrigue future historians.

Lindsay Almond had few intimate friends, and there was a
tendency on the part of other champions of massive resistance,
now that the shells were bursting, to let him ride out in front
alone. He took counsel with few, but he leaned heavily on one
faithful companion. Albertis S. Harrison, Jr., the urbane, tact-
ful and astute Attorney General, was his constant adviser. And
Harrison's advice was on the side of prudence.

If the Governor foresaw the collapse of massive resistance,
he clearly wanted it to be recorded that he "fought to the last
ditch and then dug another ditch" in defense of it. He wanted
to be able to say that he "walked the last mile, and the last
inch."

The theory that Almond was conscious of the fact that massive resistance must ultimately fall is strengthened by a step
taken at his direction on September 13. It had been considered
by the Governor and Harrison for some time and had been
hinted at earlier.

The state initiated a suit which amounted to asking the
Virginia Supreme Court of Appeals to rule that the school-
closing and fund-cut-off laws were constitutional and valid,
but which opened the door for the state court to examine all
the constitutional questions involved in the massive resistance
legislation and to deliver a contrary opinion. The Attorney

General filed a writ of mandamus against State Comptroller Sidney C. Day, Jr., to require the latter to issue warrants for tuition grants.

Day, to bring the issue before the court, had refused to authorize the payment of tuition grants to pupils attending private schools. The Supreme Court of Appeals appointed Samuel H. Williams, a Lynchburg attorney and president of the Virginia State Bar Council, to represent the Comptroller and to marshal arguments to prove that the tuition-grant law and the related fund-cut-off and school-closing laws were unconstitutional.

Harrison explained:

The procedure we are following is in our opinion, not only proper, but the quickest way to secure a determination of the issues. Furthermore, it is consistent with the policy that Virginia has followed since this crisis was precipitated by the decision of the Supreme Court of the United States in May, 1954, to meet the problem openly and to combat it as best we can in every legal, constitutional and honorable way.

Coming on the day after the closing of the Warren County High School, the announcement aroused only secondary public interest. It was pointed out in some quarters that the action in the State Supreme Court of Appeals would fend off attacks in federal courts and amount at least to another delaying gambit. Federal courts usually have taken the position that federal courts should wait and let the state courts deal first with the constitutionality of state laws.

More important in Almond's design, one may conclude in retrospect, was the consideration that it would be easier to retreat from massive resistance on a signal from Virginia's highest tribunal than in obedience to federal court orders.

18. THE NEW ISSUE—PUBLIC EDUCATION

SLOWLY the issue of public education began to transcend the race question, and courage came to Virginia moderates.

In bewildered Warren County on the day after its high school was closed, the Front Royal Ministerial Association issued a statement, which thirteen of its fourteen members signed. Church bodies in Virginia on numerous occasions had called for compliance with the desegregation ruling on moral grounds—with distressingly little effect. These Warren clergymen made only a fleeting reference to "a pattern of life which opposes the very nature of the Church as the Body of Christ." They said in part:

> The overriding issue before us is not whether we agree with a court order requiring the end of segregation. The overriding issue is the urgency of keeping our public schools open. The education of our children is at stake. . . .
>
> We have heard many people say that, while they believe in segregated schools, they would prefer schools to be kept open, even if some changes are necessary in pupil assignment. The alternative of no public schools is unthinkable!

Here was the formula for a successful movement. It was already the platform of the burgeoning Committees for Public Schools. Moderates were now able to assert themselves without advocating that thing so charged with odium—"integration." People could be asked to stand up and be counted merely as for, or against, public schools. And what could be more respectable than to defend public schools? Along this path Virginia was at last to climb out of the massive resistance miasma.

But what organization could mobilize the moderate forces?

The Norfolk ministerial association met on the day schools closed in that city. Of the seventy-four Protestant ministers present, sixty-six signed an appeal "to the leaders of our city and commonwealth to take immediate steps to reopen our schools." However, although somewhat more effective now, the clergy generally had deplored massive resistance all along.

The board of directors of the Virginia division of the American Association of University Women sent a telegram to Governor Almond, saying: "We urge that you call a special session of the General Assembly to enact realistic laws that will reopen closed schools and that will keep open the public schools now in operation." The League of Women Voters urged Virginians to express their views "openly and firmly by letter, telegram and word-of-mouth to city or county officials, to state legislators and to the governor." But these two organizations had an intellectual flavor and limited influence, and they had leaned toward compliance with the law of the land in the first place. Moreover, the members of the League were by no means unanimous in support of its liberal position. The executive committee of the AFL-CIO in Virginia distributed pamphlets opposing massive resistance; but labor was also divided, and Virginia politicians are singularly allergic to agitation from this quarter.

A very large element of Virginia's most substantial citizens are enrolled in Rotary, Kiwanis and Lions Clubs and the like, and in chambers of commerce, but they were dedicated to work for crippled children, the blind, etc., and the improvement of business. Even such an emergency as the incipient disintegration of the public school system could not be expected to divert these groups from their routine and noncontroversial endeavors.

The Parent-Teacher Associations, of course, had a vital stake in the existence of public schools. An outcry from the

state organization of P-TA's would indeed have given the
massive resistance leaders pause; even a mild gesture from that
highly representative group would have had—and did later
have—a marked effect upon the course of events. But for
several reasons the P-TA's were far from prepared to be the
spearhead of a statewide save-the-schools movement. To begin
with, many of their members, and some of their strategically
placed leaders, were openly in favor of closing public schools
rather than permitting them to be integrated. Moreover, the
P-TA's in Virginia are traditionally loyal to state policy and
seldom concern themselves with controversial matters other
than minor problems of the particular school with which each
is connected. P-TA's had striven nervously—and thus far
successfully—to avoid the desegregation issue, with all its
meaning for public schools.

The situation demanded an organization exclusively devoted
to saving the public schools, and the Committees for Public
Schools moved into the breach. These groups found their
initial inspiration and example in alert and liberal Arlington
County. We have already noted the rapid development during
the summer of the Arlington Committee to Preserve Public
Schools. The name had now been shortened to "Committee for
Public Schools." Though that county was out of immediate
danger of school-closing, its Committee went forward with
unflagging enthusiasm in preparation for a possible crisis the
following February. Committee leaders were anxious, too, to
spread the movement and arouse the state.

Spirited rallies had been held and preliminary steps had been
taken also during the summer months looking toward the
organization of Committees for Public Schools in Charlottesville and Norfolk. Committees were formally organized in
those cities on September 14 and 16. The Charlottesville group
quickly reached a membership of 1,000.

Courage, or caution, was still required to be identified even with this degree of revolt against massive resistance. When the *Norfolk Virginian-Pilot* of September 19 announced the organization of the Norfolk Committee for Public Schools, it named six members of the executive committee and added, "another member who requested that his name be not disclosed." Committee leaders were often dismayed by the refusal of normally public-spirited citizens to join their ranks. Businessmen were particularly hesitant. Many citizens, nonetheless, rallied openly around the Norfolk Committee. Clergymen, professional men, educators, office workers on the middle management level, government employees, Armed Services personnel—and their wives—were conspicuous among them. Physicians were particularly active in the movement.

The Committee placed a nearly page-size advertisement in each of Norfolk's two daily newspapers on September 24 and 25 and opened a downtown office, manned by volunteer workers. The advertisement stated the Committee's purpose, carried the names of 150 prominent supporters and invited others of like mind to become members. Women volunteers conducted a house-to-house canvass. By early November the Committee had reached a membership of 6,500.

In Warren County, where the federal court action had been swift and unexpected, no organization concerned with any aspect of the desegregation problem previously existed, except a local unit of the NAACP. Two nights after the school-closing, a dozen citizens met to look into the matter of forming a Committee for Public Schools. Four of these conferred a few days later with leaders of the Arlington, Charlottesville and Norfolk Committees in Richmond; and, upon their return to Front Royal, a Warren County Committee for Public Schools was organized, with an initial membership of eighty-seven.

This Richmond conference marked the beginning of inter-

Committee action. It was followed on November 8 by a meeting which was attended by seventeen representatives of the
four existing Committees, together with interested citizens
from Alexandria, Fairfax County, Lynchburg and Richmond.
The latter meeting looked toward the setting up of a state-
wide organization, and Dr. J. L. Blair Buck, who threw himself vigorously into the movement at this point, was asked to
serve as temporary coordinator. Dr. Buck was a former official
of the State Department of Education, who had retired in 1956,
with a sharp denunciation of the state's massive resistance
policy.

In Norfolk, the City Council of Parent-Teacher Associations
urged that no P-TA unit should take a stand on the school-
closing issue; but Norfolk P-TA's became embroiled in the
controversy notwithstanding. The P-TA Council president,
W. I. McKendree, was a member of the Defenders of State
Sovereignty, and other extreme segregationists were prominent in the organization. Some of these held that the closing
of schools also extinguished the P-TA's of those schools.
Nevertheless, most of the Norfolk P-TA units expressed
themselves in some form in favor of re-opening the schools.
The P-TA of Walter Herron Taylor Elementary School
voted 159 to four in favor of re-opening the schools. When
the officers of the P-TA of Northside Junior High, one
of the closed schools, temporized, 600 irate parents gathered
in an informal rally to urge the re-opening of that school.

P-TA disinvolvement on the state level also broke down at
last. When the Virginia Congress of Parents and Teachers met
in annual convention in Richmond on October 20–22, the race-
and-school issue overshadowed everything else. On the first
day, massive resistance sentiment was noisily manifested when
a fiery anti-integration speech by Governor Almond drew
whoops and cheers, with eleven interruptions for applause.

But the following day moderate sentiment was tenuously, yet with immense significance, in the ascendancy.

The state P-TA administration was opposed to school-closing. When the massive resistance faction sought to replace these officers with a slate of candidates nominated from the floor, the move was defeated by a two to one vote. The crucial test came on the third day of the convention when two resolutions dealing directly with the desegregation issue were offered. The first called for support of the massive resistance policy; needing a majority to pass, it was defeated by a tie vote of 557 to 557. The next resolution, one urging local option, passed by a majority of 515 to 513. Though supported by barely more than half of the convention delegates, such a gesture from the traditionally unobtrusive P-TA's gave a major jolt to the massive resistance politicians.

They were jolted again when the white public school teachers acted. These public servants, who receive part of their salary from the state, usually also are timorous about criticizing state policy. Meeting now in the annual convention of the Virginia Education Association on October 30, the teachers adopted overwhelmingly a resolution expressing "grave concern" and urging the Governor to call a special session of the legislature to insure continued operation of the public schools.

As we noted earlier, the massive resistance legislation left one obscure loophole through which a closed school might conceivably be permitted to re-open and operate on an integrated basis. This might happen if the school board and the governing board of the locality should unite in petitioning the governor, and if the latter should then, in his discretion, concur. However, if all these hurdles were surmounted, other massive resistance legislation would have cut off state funds and the community would have been left with the necessity of raising extra funds locally for school operation. It was not

an attractive recourse, but the Committees for Public Schools
in the affected localities felt that no stone should be left un-
turned.

In Arlington, the wealthiest Virginia county and the least
dependent upon state financial aid, the two boards were apparently prepared to attempt this form of immediate relief had
any Arlington schools been closed. Then, if the point had been
reached of actually depriving that county of its normal share
of state funds, the outcry could have led to something like a
taxpayer's strike—while federal courts undoubtedly would
have made short shrift of this flagrant denial of equal protection of the laws. Massive resistance, as we have noted, was
spared this explosion.

In Warren County, which was quickly engrossed in an apparently successful movement to set up private schools, the
two timid boards gave little thought to any such bold approach
to the Governor. In Charlottesville, the two boards decided
against petitioning the Governor, in the belief that the situation would right itself before long in some other way. Any
such action in Norfolk was precluded by the attitude of the
Norfolk city administration. Nor was there evidence in the
confused situation that a majority of the people in either of
these three localities favored an uncertain attempt to get the
closed schools re-opened at the cost of both integration and a
heavy new financial burden.

In Norfolk the school board had invited the city council to
join it in petitioning the Governor, and the council was under
some pressure from Committee for Public Schools leaders,
clergymen and others to do so. There was heavy support on the
other hand for the city council's adamant position. Norfolk at
this stage was torn with bitter dissension. It was not, in the
fall of 1958, a pleasant city in which to live. As moderate elements moved into the open, the extreme segregationists were

spurred to maximum activity. There was a heavy flow of "hate literature," both flyers and direct mail, into Norfolk homes. The *Norfolk Ledger-Dispatch* reported that the Defenders of State Sovereignty were "saturating Norfolk residents with a barrage of home-delivered literature." It said: "An estimated 30,000 packages of the literature have already found their way to Norfolk doorsteps."

In early November the pro-massive-resistance city council hit upon a specious means of answering those who advocated petitioning the Governor to re-open the closed schools on an integrated basis. It decided to submit the proposal to the voters; but the ballot would carry the printed warning that, if schools should be so re-opened, state funds would be cut off and parents would have to pay "substantial tuition" for each child attending school. In a referendum on November 18 this proposition was rejected by a vote of approximately three to two. Only some 22,000 of the city's 300,000 inhabitants went to the polls.

In the meantime, the Norfolk Committee for Public Schools had taken a step of fateful portent for massive resistance. Consideration had been given to several forms of legal action in federal court to force the re-opening of the city's closed schools. Attorneys for the seventeen Negro pupils who had been ordered enrolled with white pupils withdrew an earlier petition for this relief, when Federal District Judge Walter E. Hoffman informed them that they were proceeding against the wrong parties in naming the members of the school board only, and filed suit, naming Governor Almond as a defendant. The parents of a single white pupil also filed suit.

But the litigation which was to be followed through was one promoted and financed by the Norfolk Committee for Public Schools. In this suit, filed October 27, twenty-six white Norfolk residents, including eleven children, challenged the school-closing law on the ground that closing certain Norfolk schools, while permitting schools to operate elsewhere in the state, deprived the plaintiffs and others in Norfolk of equal protection of the laws. This became the crucial case of *James v. Almond*. Up to this point all the suits in the desegregation controversy in the South had been brought in behalf of Negro plaintiffs. Here for the first time was a suit in behalf of approximately 10,000 pupils, all but seventeen of whom were white.

On December 6, seventy-five leaders in the movement came to Richmond from fourteen cities and counties and formed a state organization which was to be called the Virginia Committee for Public Schools. The state Committee opened an office in Richmond under the direction of Temporary Coordinator Buck, and went to work immediately.

19. THE PRESS SOUNDS DEFEAT

IN ALL of Virginia's gyrations and turmoil over the desegregation issue the press of the state had played a peculiarly conspicuous part. Once state policy pointed toward resistance, nearly all of the press had fallen into line with it. There were fewer voices of moderation in the Virginia press than in that of any other state outside of South Carolina and the Gulf states of Alabama, Mississippi and Louisiana.

The *Norfolk Virginian-Pilot* was the one major Virginia newspaper which from the first eloquently and consistently urged compliance with the law of the land. The *Virginian-*

Pilot hailed the Supreme Court ruling of May 31, 1955, as a "superb appeal to the wisdom, intelligence and leadership of the Southern States," and called upon Virginia to "rise to leadership in the probably long and difficult task." It opposed massive resistance in an unflagging stream of cogent editorials.

But Norfolk, in spite of being Virginia's largest city, is situated in the southeastern corner of the state, and the circulation of its newspapers, though intense in the great port area, does not compare with the distribution range of the Richmond newspapers in the state as a whole.

The comment of the *Richmond News Leader* on that same 1955 ruling of the Supreme Court was typical of the kind of frenzy which characterized many of this paper's editorials. The successor to the editorial chair of Douglas Freeman wrote on June 1, 1955:

For let this be said once more, in unmistakable language: In May of 1954, that inept fraternity of politicians and professors known as the United States Supreme Court chose to throw away the established law. Those nine men repudiated the Constitution, spit upon the tenth amendment and rewrote the fundamental law of the land to suit their own gauzy concepts of sociology. . . .

To defy the court openly would be to enter upon anarchy: the logical end would be a second attempt at secession from the Union. And, though the idea is not without merit, it is impossible of execution. We tried that once before.

The *Richmond Times-Dispatch,* whose editor, Virginius Dabney, previously had been regarded as an outstanding Southern liberal, nevertheless took a gloomy and hostile attitude toward the desegregation ruling and harmonized at a lower pitch with its afternoon contemporary.

The afternoon *Ledger-Dispatch* in Norfolk was similarly hostile. The two Roanoke newspapers were more restrained in their support of massive resistance and the Lynchburg papers were early critics of that policy. In Arlington County, the *Northern Virginia Sun* came into strong and liberal hands and attained substantial circulation during this period. The three Washington newspapers, with large circulation in northern Virginia, were critical in varying degrees of Virginia's massive resistance policy; the *Washington Post and Times-Herald* opposed it aggressively.

Most Virginia newspapers, accustomed to routine support of the dominant political organization, were loath to oppose any policy firmly laid down by Senator Byrd.

The influence of the two Richmond newspapers was formidable. Published in the state capital, they were read daily by state officials, and eagerly by members of the state legislature during sessions of that body. Many politicians in all sections of the state read one of these two papers; and what is particularly significant, they served the Fourth District and the race-conscious Black Belt. The *Richmond News Leader* and its editor, Kilpatrick, had become so influential in political circles that they were widely credited with "calling the turns" in Richmond.

In October and November, 1958, rather suddenly and in a manner which suggested something like a concerted deployment of editorial force, most of the press turned sharply against massive resistance. The Lynchburg *News* and the Lynchburg *Daily Advance* became aggressively critical of the school-closing adventure. A minor sensation was caused when the *Roanoke Times* and the *Roanoke World News* declared that the time had come for a change. The Norfolk afternoon *Ledger-Dispatch*, which, unlike the *Virginian-Pilot*, had supported massive resistance, and the Charlottesville *Daily Progress* joined the procession. (The newspapers of Newport News and Petersburg, the two cities of heaviest Negro population, stood fast for massive resistance.)

On November 11, editor Kilpatrick addressed the Richmond Rotary Club. As late as October 22 the *Richmond News Leader* had said: "This is a time, we would submit, for holding firm. . . ." To 225 Rotarians and their guests the *News Leader's* editor now predicted that the federal courts, if not the Virginia Supreme Court of Appeals, soon would nullify the massive resistance laws and said that Virginia should promptly adopt new legislation.

"I believe that the new laws must be devised," Kilpatrick said "—speedily devised—if educational opportunities are to be preserved and social calamity is to be averted."

He recognized the possibility that "some public schools in Virginia ultimately may be coerced into some degree of integration," and presented a tentative plan, which included local option by referendum on school-closing.

It was a meager concession on its face, but coming from the father of modern interposition and the loudest and angriest trumpeter of massive resistance, it sounded like a bugle call to retreat.

The *Richmond Times-Dispatch* echoed the call for a new policy the next morning and the *News Leader* followed through editorially in the tenor of Kilpatrick's speech. Reporters who hastened to Governor Almond for comment were told that the Governor intended to appoint a commission to formulate a new policy in the event the massive resistance laws should be invalidated by the courts. "I am going to stay with the statutes of Virginia as long as they are vital," Almond said, but the usual denial of any mitigation of massive resistance was not forthcoming.

Said Senator Byrd: "I have supported the strong anti-integration school policy of Governor Almond and his firm stand against usurpation of power by the Warren Supreme Court. I shall continue to support this policy. . . ."

On November 20 Almond said further that Virginia might have to yield to the "overriding power" of the federal government; though he said the assignment of some Negro children to white schools would not mean the fight was over. "The fight has just begun," he said.

The anxious board of directors of the Defenders of State Sovereignty and Individual Liberties, meeting in Richmond on December 3, expressed "gravest concern," and urged: "Since Virginia . . . is the battleground upon which the eternal fight for the liberties of America must be waged, let us not falter, let us not yield."

The incident was hailed by uninhibited observers in the national press, and by many Virginians, as the beginning of the end of massive resistance.

20. BYRD AND ALMOND

As WAS to be expected after the emotional effusions which accompanied his threatened retirement the previous February, Byrd was easily re-elected on November 4. He had conducted no campaign.

The Virginia Republican Party offered no opposition. A lady candidate, Dr. Louise Wensel, had entered the race on an anti-massive-resistance platform. Rebuffed by the Republican State Central Committee, Dr. Wensel ran as an independent. With an organization consisting of a single "manager," she made a gallant but forlorn fight. A perennial Social Democratic candidate, Clarke T. Robb, also entered the race.

The vote was: Byrd, 317,221; Wensel, 120,224; Robb, 20,154. In the Tenth Congressional District (which includes Arlington County) and in Norfolk and Charlottesville, there was a marked falling off in the Byrd following. Compared with the results of the 1952 election, Byrd's percentage of the total vote in the Tenth District shrank from 74.5 to 52 per cent. The anti-Byrd vote increased in Norfolk from 29 to 40 per cent, and in Charlottesville from 17 to 34 per cent.

But the anti-Byrd vote in the state as a whole was only about "normal." The image of Byrd as a great former governor and a towering member of the United States Senate was more familiar to the general public than his role as the architect of massive resistance. His personal popularity had been little impaired.

Governor Almond, commenting on Byrd's election, said the voters had endorsed overwhelmingly both "his stand on the school situation" and his "great record of public service."

A state of strained co-existence was now evident, nevertheless, in the relations between Byrd and Almond. Apart from any actual policy differences, the sheer fact that Almond was in the driver's seat and Byrd was playing a secondary role in a critical period of Virginia's history was enough to place their relations on a precarious footing. Almond never consulted Byrd in the manner of former governors; the decisions now were Almond's own. A growing divergence in their attitudes on the school question was also perceptible in November. Almond was beginning to suggest faintly that a change of policy might be necessary; Byrd remained adamant in his insistence upon massive resistance.

As is often the case, the rumors of a rift were best confirmed by a denial. In the Governor's press conference of November 20 a reporter said:

"There have been some suggestions of a conflict between you and Senator Byrd over school policy, and that a struggle may develop between you for control of the Democratic organization. Would you comment on these reports?"

Almond replied:

No man living in Virginia has more deeply my respect and admiration than Senator Byrd. . . . There is no conflict, express or implied, between Senator Byrd and myself, and as far as I know there is not going to be any. . . . I have no ambition to take over what they call the organization and be the political kingpin of Virginia. . . .

Almond had said little publicly since the school-closing in September. This was his first regular press conference in six weeks. Commenting on a state Senator's proposal that Negro schools should be closed in communities where white schools were closed, the Governor said:

I know of many people who feel that for every white school closed, one or more Negro schools should close. I have never harbored any feeling of retaliation. . . . I want to see as many children as possible, both white and colored, receive the best we can offer in educational facilities and opportunities. . . .

Incidentally, a reporter called attention to the long absence of the national flag from its customary pole over the state Capitol, where the Virginia flag now waved alone in the breeze. Almond said that the national flag would be hoisted again as soon as a second halyard could be erected. "I respect, I worship the flag of my country," the Governor said, but he declared that the state-owned buildings would not be permitted to fly the United States flag over the Virginia flag. State and national flags should be displayed at equal levels, with preference given the state flag when only one staff was available.

These remarks punctuated a week of flag pyrotechnics, which pleased some, amused many and aroused some angry comment. The Governor insisted that his action was unrelated to the segregation controversy, but coinciding with the first rumors of a retreat from massive resistance, it had the appearance at least of a diversionary maneuver. It would surely be an indication that no one was more devoted to the principle of state rights than Lindsay Almond.

State and local officials responsible for public buildings throughout the commonwealth, from school principals to police officers, were uneasy. But few, if any, United States flags were moved. The national guard armories, with only one flagpole each, flew only the national flag; Adjutant General Sheppard Crump said: "We've been doing this for years and at the moment we have no plans to change." Major W. C. Thomas said state police facilities would continue to fly the American flag until a directive to the contrary was received from the Governor. Public schools still flew the United States flag at the top of their flagpoles and the Virginia flag underneath.

Even the return of the national flag to Virginia's historic Capitol was expedited. Five days after the Governor's remark, without waiting for the erection of an additional central flagpole, the state flag was moved to the House of Delegates wing of the Capitol and the Stars and Stripes waved over the Senate wing—at the right, as prescribed in the flag display rules laid down by Congress.

Columnist Charles McDowell wrote in the *Richmond Times-Dispatch:*

> O! Say, can you see by the dawn's early light,
> Is it up, is it down, since the twilight's last gleaming?
> Is the flag of the state at a similar height?
> Are both of them there, so co-equally streaming?
> After video's glare, the bombast in air,
> Is it clear that the flags are now dually there?
> O! Say that our far-wrangled banners at last,
> Are secure, and this Capitol tempest is passed.

21. MASSIVE RESISTANCE ON TRIAL

BRIEFS and oral argument were presented by opposing counsel in November and early December, 1958, in the two suits, one in the Supreme Court of Appeals of Virginia and the other in a three-judge federal district court, testing the validity of massive resistance laws under the state and the federal constitution respectively.

The latter suit, *James* v. *Almond*, was, as we have noted, a rare instance of a momentous litigation involving the question of school segregation in which neither the NAACP nor any Negro had a direct part. In a four-hour hearing on November 19 before Circuit Judges Simon E. Soboloff and Clement F. Haynsworth, Jr. and District Judge Walter E. Hoffman, the attorneys for the plaintiffs, Edmund D. Campbell and Archie L. Boswell, held that denying education to 10,000 Norfolk students while providing free public education under general law was a denial of equal protection of the laws. They said also that it constituted "an evasive scheme designed to nullify orders issued by the Federal district courts."

Campbell, an eminent attorney and leader in the Committee for Public Schools movement, had come to Norfolk from Arlington County to argue the case. He said that the designation of which schools should close was based on race and color alone and therefore "patently unconstitutional." He recognized a certain problem in Norfolk, but said: "I don't believe, in the absence of inflammatory action, the admission of seventeen Negro children would cause any difficulty."

Boswell emphasized denial of equal protection of the laws, and said the injury to the 10,000 Norfolk children was so severe that the court should not await a decision of the State

Supreme Court of Appeals. Boswell expressed his opinion that
no relief would come from the Virginia court.

Four witnesses testified that the situation in Norfolk would
be tragic unless the schools re-opened soon. They included:
J. J. Brewbaker, Superintendent of Schools; E. L. Lambert, an
assistant superintendent; Paul Schweitzer, chairman of the
school board; and Miss Mary Johnson, a teacher at the closed
Granby High School. Lambert estimated that between 2,500
and 3,000 Norfolk children were without any kind of instruction as a result of the closings. Schweitzer said dozens of
teachers were asking for advice as to what they should do. If
they should leave Norfolk, the effect would be disastrous.

Attorney General Harrison and his special assistant, Walter E.
Rogers, appeared for the defendants, who were named as the
Governor and Attorney General of Virginia, the Norfolk Superintendent of Schools, the Norfolk school board and the
individual members of that board. Harrison said that the
school-closing law was not a scheme designed to evade desegregation orders, but a measure of precaution against such
violence as had occurred in other Southern states.

The state's argument deviated in several respects from or-
thodox massive resistance doctrine. Rogers, under questioning,
indicated that the schools in Norfolk might be re-opened upon
a favorable decision by the State Supreme Court of Appeals on
the constitutionality of the tuition grant laws. Harrison also
suggested that it might be possible for the Governor to permit the re-opening of the schools if tuition grants were available for those who objected to attending integrated public
schools.

Rogers said "the laws [the massive resistance package]
clearly contemplate integrated schools will be operated."

Early in November opposing counsel filed briefs in the state
Supreme Court of Appeals in the case of *Harrison* v. *Day*. This

was the action initiated by the state administration to test the
constitutionality of the massive resistance legislation on the
question of releasing tuition grants. The validity of the proposed payments depended on whether the Virginia constitution
was violated by the state statutes, designed to prevent public
school integration, under which a school, upon being integrated, would be closed and state funds cut off from that
school would be used for tuition grant payments for the education of the displaced pupils in nonsectarian private schools.
By petitioning for a writ of mandamus to compel Comptroller
Day to issue warrants for tuition grant disbursements, the
Almond administration had posed a test case involving the
constitutionality of the package of massive resistance laws.

Attorney General Harrison and Assistant Attorney General
Robert D. McIlwaine III virtually staked their case upon the
theory, earlier advanced in the General Assembly debates,
that all public school mandates were eliminated from the Virginia constitution by the Supreme Court's school desegregation
decree. Section 129 of the Virginia constitution provides: "The
General Assembly shall establish and maintain an efficient system of public free schools throughout the state." Section 140
says: ". . . white and colored children shall not be taught in
the same school." The attorneys for the state administration
told the court that, when the United States Supreme Court
struck down Section 140, it automatically struck down 129.
Even if 129 is still valid, they continued, the General Assembly
can define what is an "efficient" school system, and the
Assembly had said that no school attended by members of both
races can be an efficient school.

But Williams, the attorney appointed by the court to oppose
the state, insisted that Section 129 still stood and that the fund
cut-off and school-closing measures were in violation of that
section. He said the U. S. Supreme Court merely modified Sec-

tion 129 to add, in effect these words "from which no person otherwise qualified may be barred on account of race."

Williams charged that the anti-integration laws violated the state constitution in that they (1) deprived local school boards of the right to operate public schools, (2) applied state funds for the unequal benefit of all the people of the state, and (3) deprived local school boards of the right to spend local school funds according to their judgment. In view of the mandates of Section 129 and other sections which deal with local control rights, Williams said, the anti-integration laws must fall.

The arguments were repeated orally in a two and one-half hour hearing on November 24, in which McIlwaine bore the brunt of the questioning. Chief Justice John W. Eggleston agreed with McIlwaine that the United States Supreme Court could not change the Virginia high court's interpretation of the state constitution, although it could overrule the state court on federal constitutional questions. Eggleston, whose twenty-three years as associate justice had been distinguished by a firm respect for the letter of the law, had been named chief justice the previous summer.

The questioning in this state court, however, dealt extensively with the Fourteenth Amendment of the United States Constitution and the Supreme Court rulings. Chief Justice Eggleston asked how the state met the argument that its laws constituted an "evasive scheme" in the sense of the recent ruling in the Little Rock case.

McIlwaine dismissed the Supreme Court's pronouncement as a "mass of gratuitous dicta," without specific reference to situations like that in Virginia. Associate Justice A. C. Buchanan pursued the questioning, quoting the Little Rock ruling's condemnation of any evasive scheme to continue segregation, and its warning that state support of segregated schools "through any arrangement, management, funds or property" violated the Fourteenth Amendment. "If we're bound by that in this case, doesn't that foreclose the question?" Justice Buchanan asked.

McIlwaine thought it did not, saying tuition grants could be used for integrated as well as segregated private schooling and that voluntary segregation was permissible.

Chief Justice Eggleston wanted to know if closing some schools and leaving others open did not violate the equal-protection clause of the Fourteenth Amendment. To this McIlwaine replied that the school-closing was only "temporary." In this connection, Attorney General Harrison pointed to disorders in Little Rock and elsewhere and asked: "Isn't it better to close schools a while rather than incur violence and disorder?"

22. THE BUSINESSMEN MOVE

AN UNFORTUNATE feature of the desegregation problem in the South has been the stubborn insistence of most business leaders, whose pragmatic approach would be a healthy antidote to prevailing hysteria, upon keeping as far away as possible from the controversy. Businessmen are inclined to rationalize that this is a matter for the politicians, the preachers, the professors or the editors—that their concern is only with manufacturing plastics, operating the banks or selling automobiles.

When schools actually close, as we saw in Little Rock, the business community discovers that business itself is directly and critically concerned; and it moves tardily, but with telling effect. Yet until the shock is registered, and until also there is assurance of unity among them, the attitude of business leaders generally is one of apparent apathy. Unity is important; when businessmen finally assert themselves, the magic number of 100 is likely to be sought in securing signatures to a public statement.

Businessmen are frightened in the first instance by the singular malevolence of the segregationist agitation. This silences many voices of moderation in all walks of life. City and state employees fear political reprisals; doctors and lawyers fear the effect on their practices; small merchants fear the loss of trade; ministers fear divided congregations; and all fear subtle social pressure or outright abuse. Corporation executives find further excuse for disinvolvement in their responsibility to stockholders and directors.

These considerations were present in the silence with which men of large affairs in Virginia watched the trend toward demoralization of the public school system. The latter were also influenced in this state by the particularly close relationship between business and the dominant political organization, and the reluctance of business leaders to set themselves against any policy advanced by Senator Byrd.

Businessmen were naturally wary of identification with such an openly anti-segregation organization as the Council on Human Relations. But many refused at the beginning to support even the Committees for Public Schools, which sought to by-pass the segregation issue itself, and concentrated solely on saving the public schools. Not until the climax of the fight in January were large numbers of prominent businessmen willing openly to insist that the public school system be preserved.

But when massive resistance began to express itself in the cold reality of closed schools, many business leaders did become aroused; privately they expressed growing concern.

Their feeling was not unknown to newspaper publishers and editors; and though no business executive spoke out, their influence was felt by the political confraternity.

Dr. Lorin Thompson, not a businessman but an economist from the University of Virginia faculty, published a paper which admirably expressed what was already in the minds of some businessmen and offered food for thought for others. His paper was entitled, "Some Economic Aspects of Virginia's Current Educational Crisis."

Dr. Thompson dealt primarily with the proposition of a general abandonment of the public schools but it was apt also with reference to such steps in that direction as had already been taken. This economist pointed out that abandonment of the public school system would necessitate the liquidation of all school property; and that the holders of school bonds in excess of $200 million would require immediate settlement. If the proceeds of the sale in any locality should be less than the outstanding indebtedness, the local government would have to increase taxes to make up this deficit. Private school enthusiasts were reminded that the financial underwriting necessary for the acquisition of public school property valued at $600 million would be a formidable undertaking. He predicted that in the confusion in Virginia the rapid population growth and shortage of teachers elsewhere would siphon off a substantial portion of the qualified teachers in this state.

More pertinently to the immediate situation, Dr. Thompson wrote:

The higher cost of private schooling would unquestionably have the effect of encouraging families who now work in manufacturing plants, business concerns and professional services in Virginia to move to other states. . . .

An increasing number of the new industries in Virginia are having difficulties in bringing into their plants the highly trained personnel needed to guide production and distribution programs. Some skilled workers in these plants and industries have already left because they regarded the education of their children to be of paramount importance. They have returned to places where the situation is more dependable and stable than in Virginia. As more schools become subject to Federal court orders to desegregate, more and more communities in Virginia will be affected by this kind of situation. . . . Any environment which is unstable and in which public education is threatened is not conducive to business development or expansion.

Statistical items such as the report that it was costing the state $172,000 a month (chiefly in pay for idle teachers) just to keep schools closed in Norfolk also made little sense to hard-headed businessmen.

The fact that Virginia was already suffering economic penalties of public school trouble was becoming apparent in November. The statement was repeatedly made among business groups that not a single new industry had opened a plant in Virginia during 1958; and, though not literally so, this statement was substantially correct. Business was not bad in Virginia. Public utilities and some long-established manufacturing plants had carried out large expansion programs during the year. But new industries were holding back. The year's statistical reports were to show that, while a number of very small new plants had opened during the year, the total number of persons employed in them was less than the number displaced when several larger plants closed.

Attention was called to the sensational industrial progress in North Carolina, where no schools had closed or were in danger of closing.

Concerned business leaders moved quietly, indeed with a degree of secrecy, during November. Informal meetings were held, culminating early in December in a dinner conference with the Governor, who was accompanied by the Attorney

General and Lieutenant-Governor A. E. S. Stephens. None of these activities were reported in the press, and I shall refrain from mentioning the names of participants here (although local business leaders in Charlottesville and Norfolk were later to give their protest public expression). When businessmen were invited to these state-wide meetings, they were assured that their names would be withheld, and no essentially useful purpose would be served by disclosing them. It is significant, however, that a policy of privacy in this particular proved successful. It may be confidently stated that Virginia business leaders finally brought vigorous and effective pressure, of which the public was not aware, to bring massive resistance to an end.

At the climactic state-wide meeting, twenty-nine businessmen, industrialists and bankers from various sections, representing to an impressive degree the economic power structure of Virginia, sat down to dinner with Almond, Stephens and Harrison in the Rotunda Club in Richmond. No one said in so many words: "This nonsense has gone far enough," but the state's business leaders expressed their urgent concern. At some points the conversation became heated. The Governor replied that he had merely complied with Virginia law and that there was nothing he could do, at least until the courts had ruled on the pending questions. He was noncommittal and apparently even uncooperative. But he carried back to the Executive Mansion a new awareness of the imperatives of the public school crisis.

23. THE PRIVATE SCHOOL EXPERIMENT

BY THE end of 1958 it was possible to get an idea of how far the private school improvisations had filled the gap in the public school system. Many massive resistance enthusiasts had predicted that a changeover from public to private education would offer no insuperable problem, and that children leaving public schools would move smoothly into private schools and pursue their education as well or better there. How well was this theory borne out during this hectic fall in Virginia?

In Warren County and Charlottesville approximately four-fifths of the displaced public school pupils had been provided for after a fashion and were receiving some kind of instruction locally; a handful had been transferred to private or public schools elsewhere, and only between 150 and 200 in each district were left entirely without schooling.

In Norfolk, despite valiant efforts on the part of an army of public-spirited citizens, the community effort had been far less successful. Less than 4,500 of the nearly 10,000 displaced pupils in that city were being accommodated in local private school classes. Approximately 948 pupils had been transferred to the public schools of the contiguous city of South Norfolk; 1,621 had been officially transferred to public or private schools outside of the area, and a few others had transferred without requesting transcripts of their records. Between 2,500 and 3,000 Norfolk children were receiving no education or tutoring of any kind.

The Tidewater Education Foundation promoted by the Defenders of State Sovereignty, which had expected to carry most of the Norfolk load of displaced pupils, had run into innumerable difficulties, due in part to its identification with those extremists. Disappointed in the refusal of active public school teachers to lend their services, its Tidewater Academy did not open until October 21, and then could take only a sixty-five-member class. It later reached an enrollment of 270 students, who were taught mainly by retired teachers. Though it was planned as a permanent institution, the Academy was holding classes temporarily in the Bayview Baptist Church in the city's Ocean View section.

Approximately 4,200 Norfolk children had been accommodated in very loosely organized tutoring classes. These were meeting now in a variety of buildings. One used a vacant store. Others met in basements, attics or living rooms of private homes. The majority met in the twenty-seven churches and synagogues that had made rooms available. Many classes had been organized simply by groups of mothers, who would bring together a dozen or two dozen children, then find a classroom and a teacher for them.

In Charlottesville, 1,384 of the 1,735 displaced pupils were in the makeshift private schools and 179 children had found schools elsewhere. The segregationist Charlottesville Educational Foundation and the pro-public-school Parents' Committee for Emergency Schooling sponsored the high school classes jointly, while each organization operated its own elementary school. Of the 1,080 students who were expected to enter Lane High School for the 1958–59 term, 862 were in the private school system. Of the 655 pupils from Venable Elementary School, 182 were attending the private Robert E. Lee School, established by the CEF in an eight-room brick dwelling, and 340 were in classes operated in private homes by the PCES.

In Warren County, 780 of the approximately 1,000 displaced high school students were provided for by a single private school organization. They used about thirty classrooms in five different buildings in downtown Front Royal—Methodist,

Baptist, and Episcopal Sunday School buildings, a museum of the United Daughters of the Confederacy and a former private home which had served as a youth center.

It is significant that the private school experiment was proving most successful in the district with the smallest number of displaced pupils, and that the difficulties appeared to multiply as the dimensions of the problem increased. In the metropolitan district of Norfolk, with 10,000 pupils to provide for, the private school improvisation had failed utterly to take the place of public schools. If the educational foundation as a non-governmental civic enterprise had been at least temporarily feasible operating as a small, compact unit, there was no indication that it would be able to cope with the staggering organizational, administrative and financial problems of large-scale operation. It was one thing to bring together public-spirited citizens to meet an urgent need in a small community where "everyone knew everyone else," and where the extent of the participation of each prominent resident was generally known; it was quite another to unite divergent elements and coordinate leadership in a city of 275,000 population.

The relative success of the Warren County project had been due only in part to the manageable dimensions of the problem there. It was aided financially by several anomalous circumstances. One of these, for instance, was a check for $16,000 from the Virginia Education Fund. Warren, being the first county to have a school closed because of threatened integration, received many donations from segregationist well-wishers elsewhere in Virginia and the South.

But Warren County's greatest financial bulwark was a local labor union. In contrast with the attitude of the state AFL-CIO, and that of the Textile Workers Union of America, Local 371 of the latter union at Front Royal took an aggressively pro-segregation position. This local, which embraced nearly all of the employees of the Front Royal plant of the American Viscose Corporation, undertook to contribute from $1,600 to $1,700 per week to the support of the private school undertaking. The money was obtained by a one-dollar-a-week check-off from the wages of each member. A feud between the local's handful of Negro members and its overwhelming white majority, and considerations of politics and community status, were factors in this extraordinary move on the part of a group which had shown mildly liberal tendencies in the past.

Unlike many of the teachers who lent their services in the tutoring classes of Charlottesville and Norfolk, all twenty-eight of the teachers in the Front Royal private school were paid regular salaries. Twenty-six of them had previously taught in the public school and had now terminated their contracts with the county school board; they were receiving the same pay as before. The private school observed the usual school hours, with 55-minute classes, from 9 A.M. to 3 P.M. It had an atmosphere of normal routine and of permanency.

In the over-all picture, the concept of limited private school accommodations to serve as a safety valve for public school desegregation had survived the four months' experience; it would endure in Virginia and in time, no doubt, would be embraced elsewhere in the South. There seemed to be a place, at least for some years to come, for private educational havens in integrated public school districts, attended by the children of parents with extreme views in the matter of race and with the means to afford the extra expense. But the impracticability of the substitution of private schools generally, or on a large scale, had been demonstrated to all but the most extreme advocates of continued complete segregation.

Aside from the administrative and other difficulties, no one had come forward with anything that resembled a practical solution of the huge financial problem. State aid in the form of tuition grants had been prevented by the litigation which the state administration had initiated to test the constitutionality of the statute. It was generally and correctly anticipated that—under new legislations if necessary—such tuition grants would eventually be available, based on the per pupil cost of public school operation. But not without large-scale development and years of established routine, if ever, would private schools be able to operate with comparable economy. There were doubts, too, if the state tuition grant principle would survive the ultimate constitutional tests. And hardly a beginning had been made on the vast problem of capital investment in buildings and equipment. The private schools were subsisting on a hand-to-mouth basis from voluntary contributions and, in Charlottesville and Norfolk, from tuition fees for pupils whose parents could afford to pay them. The ardor, not only of students and parents but of financial supporters, was sure to cool when the novelty and excitement of the experiment wore off.

Not all the reports on the private school experience were unfavorable. Small classes made more intensive instruction possible. Difficulties and hardships in some cases increased incentive. The crisis had dramatized the importance of education in a manner which bolstered the morale of parents, children and teachers alike. The absence of extra-curricular activities itself resulted in fewer classroom interruptions and more concentrated work on essential studies. One studious youngster remarked: "I'm getting a better education—there's nothing to do but study."

In the honeymoon-like glow of the experiment teachers complained little of the inconveniences and the lack of facilities and resources which were formerly at their fingertips. They were almost unanimously of the opinion that their pupils were working harder than ever before—though many of them had to write on their laps for want of desks. Teachers also found more interest and cooperation on the part of parents.

Fears of a widespread increase in juvenile delinquency were not realized. Among the several thousand high school students who were left without schooling of any kind, many had found work, some terminating their school careers at this point; some also had married. Lieutenant R. P. Racine, head of the youth bureau of the Norfolk Police Department, found that juvenile delinquency had actually decreased. This officer said later: "I think the fact that many of them attended school at night and on Saturdays helped to keep them out of trouble. I believe that the closing of the schools caused the children to realize the importance of education and sharpened their desire for it."

Miss Gaylord Gibson, an English teacher in the Warren County private school, said of her pupils: "The great majority are working more seriously and with better results. They are doing more home work. I think the jolt has made them work harder." But Miss Gibson added: "We all insist it's only temporary. We all want to get back into our high school." Another teacher said: "The children are doing fine. They aren't complaining. But I think they'll be fed up before the end of the year."

In spite of the extenuating features, a large proportion of the school patrons in Warren and Charlottesville had found the private school improvisation acceptable only as an emergency expedient. The Charlottesville Committee for Emergency Schooling insisted that its activities were temporary and urged re-opening of the public schools.

In Norfolk, despite a limited number of contented parents and pupils, conditions on the whole were clearly intolerable. Most local tutoring classes were pitifully lacking in both school equipment and ordinary living comfort. In many cases card tables took the place of desks, and students held books and papers in their laps. There were no school libraries or cafeterias, no science laboratories, no shops. There was no instruction in music or art, no physical education. The quality of teaching was miscellaneous; often pupils had to take whatever subjects a teacher could be found to teach. There was also a new expense for parents to meet in the tuition fees, averaging about $20 a month per pupil.

Classes for the 948 children attending school in South Norfolk were from 4 to 9 P.M. A Norfolk pupil attending school in a neighboring district left home in some cases at seven o'clock in the morning and took several buses to reach his school. In one Norfolk family, the oldest girl was sent to Glens Falls, New York, to stay with friends and attend the local high school; the middle child, also a daughter, was admitted to a private school in Virginia Beach, seventeen miles from Norfolk; and the youngest, a son, was taught in a local tutoring class. Another mother and father found educational refuge for their daughter with friends in Florida, while their son was placed in a military school in Georgia. Exiles from Norfolk's schools were scattered over twenty-nine states.

The three-judge federal district court in the decision in the case of *James* v. *Almond* was to say three weeks later of the Norfolk situation:

The plight of the school children and the teaching personnel who would have been in attendance at the six schools has been adequately described as "tragic." Children who would be in their last year of high school are at a loss as to what to do, and those who had planned to attend college are completely frustrated.

Of the teachers the court said:

The morale is at a low ebb; they do not know when, if ever, they will resume the noble profession of educating the youth of Virginia, to which they have dedicated their lives. . . . If the teachers leave for a more certain field of endeavor, the public of Norfolk will lose and, even if we were to assume that private tutoring groups would and could continue, the teaching source of supply would be so limited that only a scattered number of children could receive this type of education.

24. TWILIGHT OF MASSIVE RESISTANCE

DURING December, 1958, and early January, 1959, there was an inclination in most quarters to mark time in the desegregation controversy. A decision was expected from the Virginia Supreme Court of Appeals on January 19, and it was assumed the three-judge federal court would deliver its decision on the same day or shortly thereafter. The area of crisis was expanded, however, by two further developments.

The Norfolk city council in November, when it adopted the city's appropriation ordinance for 1959, had not approved the public school budget in its usual form, but had merely appropriated school funds "on a tentative basis." It had stipulated that "no part of the funds appropriated therein would be available to the school board of the city of Norfolk except as the council might from time to time, by resolution, authorize. . . ." The move was an unconcealed threat to withhold funds for the operation of Negro schools.

Moreover, in the manner in which the city council proposed to carry out the threat, a further group of white children would also have been turned out of their schools. On January 13 the city council found it "necessary for the immediate preservation of the public peace, property, health and safety" to declare that an "emergency" existed; and it refused "to authorize the payment or the transfer to the school board . . .

for use by it during the month of February, 1959, or during any month subsequent thereto" any funds for the operation of any grades above the sixth. The school board was requested to make the necessary arrangements to operate, "beginning February 21, 1959, only grades 1 through 6."

The plan would have added more than 7,000 to the 10,000 Norfolk children already locked out of public schools. Of these 5,259 would have been colored children and 1,914 white. Mayor Duckworth, whose performance at this stage resembled that of a Faubus on the city level, declared: "Seventeen Negro children are keeping 10,000 whites out of school." The move had a distinct odor of revenge.

The Norfolk Committee for Public Schools moved with dispatch. Two days later its attorneys, Campbell and Boswell, filed a suit in federal court on behalf of forty-two white children and forty-seven parents, and all those similarly situated, for temporary and permanent injunctions against enforcing the ordinance and resolutions of this plan. The suit attacked the city council's plan as an evasive and discriminatory scheme in violation of the Fourteenth Amendment. Plaintiffs said further that if it should be carried out, "the economic prosperity of the city will be ruined. Property values in the city will tumble, the citizens of Norfolk will be humiliated before the nation and the world."

Meanwhile, another Virginia school district was added to the critical list. NAACP attorneys had filed suit on September 5, seeking the admission of fourteen Negro pupils to five white schools in the city of Alexandria. In a hearing on January 13 Federal District Judge Albert V. Bryan told the Alexandria school board that it must dispose of the applications without racial discrimination and in accordance with "fair, just and valid rules and regulations," and report back to him by January 26.

The Virginia Committee for Public Schools, with a membership in the state now of 15,000, redoubled its efforts, and businessmen in Charlottesville and Norfolk at last prepared to take a public stand against massive resistance.

Francis Pickens Miller, of Charlottesville, was the anti-Byrd liberal who made the phenomenally close run for the Democratic gubernatorial nomination in 1949. In recent years he had been more conspicuously identified with church than with political affairs. He had been Presbyterian moderator of the Synod of Virginia and was at the time president of the Virginia Council of Churches and a member of the Central Committee of the World Council of Churches. Miller had been quietly active throughout most of 1958 in alerting Charlottesville business and civic leaders to the gravity of the situation. Mayor Michie, William R. Hill, the Charlottesville representative in the House of Delegates, and Knox Turnbull, a Charlottesville insurance man, were prominent in the same endeavor. President Darden of the University of Virginia met with the group from time to time.

A luncheon meeting with Miller on December 22 was significant as an indication of a bolder participation by businessmen in the movement to save the public schools. Among those present were the following: Francis P. Brawley, general manager of Miller & Rhoads, Inc.; L.D. Cooley, president, Rugby Hotel Company; David Eggenburger, managing editor, McGraw Hill Book Company; Milton L. Grigg, architect; John L. Hammond, general manager, Sperry-Piedmont Company; R. E. Lee, general contractor; and Bruce Richardson, general manager, Thomas Jefferson Inn. The same individuals met with Miller again on January 14, with the addition of William S. Hildreth, chairman of the board of the People's National Bank, and William B. Murphy and Knox Turnbull, insurance agents.

This group drew up a statement which in its final form was

headed: "A Non-Political Statement by a Group of Independent Citizens." The statement said in several paragraphs that

the vital human and economic interests of this community can best be served by reopening our public schools as soon as practicable. [It added:] WE REGISTER COMPLETE CONFIDENCE IN THE CAPACITY OF OUR LOCAL SCHOOL BOARD AND OUR LOCAL GOVERNMENT to assure the reopening and maintenance of our local public schools in such fashion as to serve the best interests of this community.

In a further "Comment," the statement said in part:

In this community we have felt the impact of school-closing. The heroic efforts to provide patchwork education deserve high praise. We are convinced, however, that the prolonged continuance of closed schools is intolerable and accordingly that it is in the interest of all our citizens to support a policy designed to reopen schools.

It was first intended to issue the manifesto over the signatures of fifty or seventy-five leading citizens, but it was later decided that mass signatures would be preferable. Actually over 1,200 signatures were secured. The statement, with only a sampling of the signatures, appeared as a newspaper advertisement on January 31.

In Norfolk, in the meantime, businessmen, who were in touch with the group in Charlottesville, were preparing a veritable power structure manifesto. This statement, in the same tenor as that of the Charlottesville group, appeared as a full-page ad on January 25, over the names of 100 of the best-known leaders of the business community. In both cities it was decided that the statements should be published only after the State Supreme Court of Appeals and the three-judge federal court had handed down their decisions.

On January 11 Governor Almond had completed one year in office. Conferring with politicians and school officials, listening to an endless stream of visitors, answering criticism, studying and drafting papers and speeches, he found that the school problem had consumed by far the greater part of his time. In no year since the 1860's had such tension, pressures, worries and hard decisions confronted a governor of Virginia. But he remained in good health, and during this mid-January lull in the storm he appeared to have achieved a certain serenity of spirit. He spent more time now in the quiet of his new library-study at the Executive Mansion—while Virginia awaited the verdict of the courts on massive resistance.

Virginians are justly proud of their own judiciary. The reputation of the state's unique political organization for producing able public servants is nowhere better justified than in the men who are chosen to preside over circuit courts or are elevated to the Supreme Court of Appeals. The seven justices who had weighed the constitutionality of the massive resistance laws—Chief Justice John W. Eggleston and Associate Justices C. Vernon Spratley, A. C. Buchanan, Kennon C. Whittle, Lawrence W. l'Anson, Willis D. Miller and Harold F. Snead—were all men of high caliber. Chief Justice Eggleston, who wrote the opinion on the massive resistance laws, was seventy-two; his associates were a little more or a little less than seventy years of age. All but one had been named to the high bench long before the beginning of the school desegregation furor in 1954. Sunday evening, January 18, following an annual custom, the Governor and Mrs. Almond were hosts to the justices of the State Supreme Court of Appeals and their wives at a dinner in the executive mansion.

January 19 was the birthday of General Robert E. Lee. This exalted circumstance escaped many even in Virginia in the transcendent events of that fateful day in 1959. For it was the day when the courts would deliver their opinions on massive resistance. But the legal holiday was not overlooked by the majority of state employees, including the custodial staff of the state Supreme Court building. The doors of that edifice were locked Monday morning, and some of the justices, all of whom arrived at about 8:30 A.M., had to knock and identify themselves to gain admission. Soon, however, the word was passed to the Capitol police to open the doors to the public, and the courtroom quickly filled to overflowing.

The session had been scheduled for 9:30 A.M.; the justices, who lingered about two hours in their conference room, did not enter the courtroom until 10:25. The decision, in its effect, was made known with a minimum of drama. Chief Justice Eggleston announced simply that in the case of *Harrison* v. *Day* the petition for mandamus was denied, with Justices Miller and Snead dissenting. Copies of the opinion, he said, would be available at the clerk's office at half past eleven o'clock. With that, newspapermen bolted, and the court turned to routine business.

The principal massive resistance laws had been stricken down!

The justices having made some minor changes in the text of the opinion during their morning conference (which necessitated re-typing several pages), copies were not actually ready for distribution until noon. It fell to John B. Boatwright, Jr., chief of the division of statutory drafting in the Capitol, to deliver the first copy to Governor Almond.

"It's a sad day, Governor," he said.

Almond, who had been waiting calmly in his office, showed no signs of dismay. He told Boatwright not to take it too hard, and smiled gently as he said, "I think we'll come out all right."

The Governor had only a few words for reporters, who gathered quickly at his office. He would have to "study the opinion very carefully." In the meantime, he would say only: "It is not necessary for me to say this, but I wish to make it very clear, I have implicit faith in, and the highest respect for, the capacity and integrity of the Supreme Court of Appeals and for each and every member thereof."

The five-to-two opinion, written by Chief Justice Eggleston, ruled that both closing schools and cutting off state funds to prevent racial integration in the public schools were in violation of the Virginia constitution. Since the tuition grants for private schooling as an alternative to integration were tied into the school-closing and fund-cut-off provisions, it declared that such tuition grants were unconstitutional and could not be paid.

The state court added:

Having reached the conclusion that certain provisions of the acts with which we are concerned violate the provisions of the Constitution of Virginia in the several respects stated, it is not necessary that we consider the question whether these acts likewise violate the provisions of the Fourteenth Amendment to the federal Constitution as interpreted by the recent decisions of the Supreme Court of the United States in *Brown* vs. *Board of Education* and *Aaron* vs. *Cooper*.

Nevertheless, the court inserted this note of sympathy with the supporters of massive resistance:

There is no occasion for us to discuss these decisions other than to say that we deplore the lack of judicial restraint evinced by that court in trespassing on the sovereign rights of this commonwealth, reserved to it in the Constitution of the United States. It was an understandable effort to diminish the evils explicit from the decision in the Brown case that prompted the enactment of the statutes now under review.

In their dissenting opinion, Justices Miller and Snead accepted the state's argument that since it was clearly intended by the framers of the constitution that public schools were to be segregated, Section 129, which requires the state to "maintain an efficient system of public free schools throughout the state" was rendered inoperative when the United States Supreme Court invalidated Section 140, requiring school segregation. The majority opinion, however, said:

We hold that Section 140 and other sections in Article IX, including Section 129, dealing with public education, are independent and separable, and that the destruction of Section 140 by the decision in the Brown case did not strike down the other provisions in Article IX.

. . . That Section [129] requires the state to "maintain an efficient system of public free schools throughout the state." That means that the state must support such public free schools in the state as are necessary to an efficient system, including those in which the pupils of both races are compelled to be enrolled and taught together, however unfortunate that situation may be.

The decision of the three-judge federal district court in Norfolk on the same day was vastly important, but it was less exciting. Segregationists had learned to expect adverse decisions from federal courts. In *James* v. *Almond*, the court listed the school-closing statutes enacted in 1956 and 1958, together with the Governor's school-closing proclamation, and declared them all "in violation of the Fourteenth Amendment to the Constitution of the United States and therefore void." As long as the state maintains a public school system, the court said, "the closing of a public school or grade therein, for the reasons heretofore assigned, violates the right of a citizen to equal protection of the laws."

As a demolition job the pronouncement was remarkable. The various individual defendants, each named, and the Norfolk school board, their successors in office, agents, etc. "and all other persons in active concert or participation with said defendants" were "permanently enjoined from in any manner, directly or indirectly, taking any steps to enforce, operate or execute or continue to recognize those statutes of the Commonwealth of Virginia. . . ."

It was announced that the Governor would speak over a
state-wide television-radio hook-up Wednesday evening, January 20 at 7:30 o'clock. He canceled his regular appointments
for Wednesday and spent the day in preparation for his broadcast.

25. SWAN SONG

GOVERNOR ALMOND's speech of January 20 was unfortunate
and indefensible. A vast number of Virginians who tuned in
their radio or television sets that evening were hoping to hear
that the war was over; they heard the Governor say instead,
amid familiar bombast and bluster: "We have just begun to
fight."

Other thousands were pleased, though a little puzzled, to
hear the Governor promise continued resistance. But for these
it was only a preparation for greater disillusionment when eight
days later Almond was to give up massive resistance. Undoubtedly there would have been fewer cries of "traitor" and
"double-crosser" when that time came if Almond had seized
this earlier opportunity to prepare the public for his imminent
change of course.

Many a Southern politician today is confronted with the
baffling question of how to loosen one's grip on the tail of the
bear. How can a leader change in time to avert disaster, not
only for his people, but for himself? Exploiting race prejudice
is, for all but the bravest and most skillful, a one-way street.
The politician who tries to turn around after leading his people

down that road must expect to see many loyal followers changed overnight into bitter and vindictive enemies; he must rely heavily on the support of moderates who have opposed him hitherto.

Almond's strategy was to blaze with defiance to the very last in the apparent hope that, when he finally declared the battle hopeless, many of his associates in massive resistance would follow him into the moderate camp. Extremists listen more readily to one of their number who reluctantly takes a moderate course than to leaders who have been moderate all the time. That concept had undoubted merit in the Virginia situation.

But Almond erred grievously in his timing. It was already too late on January 20 for that kind of speech; "the very last" had been reached the day before. It may have been his purpose to avoid Defenders demonstrations and Byrd-machine pressures in advance of the coming session of the legislature. No doubt he preferred to hold the bellicose posture until he could sound the retreat, as he was to do later in a masterly speech, standing face to face with his fellow politicians on the floor of the General Assembly.

The speech of January 20 was, nevertheless, a mistake; a year later Almond himself admitted as much. Virginius Dabney, writing in *U. S. News and World Report* of January 18, 1960, quoted Almond as saying:

> I was tired, harassed and under strain, and I wanted to reassure the people that I was doing all that I could, consistent with honor and law, to avoid that which I then considered, and now consider, a calamity. My words inadvertently gave the impression that I knew of some way to prevent any mixing of the races in the public schools, when nothing of the sort was possible.

In that fifteen-minute broadcast, Almond hurled a fierce challenge:

to those of faint heart; to those whose purpose and design is to blend and amalgamate the white and Negro race and destroy the integrity of both races; to those who disclaim that they are integrationists but are working day and night to integrate our schools; to those who don't care what happens to the children of Virginia; to those false prophets of a "little or token integration"; to those in high place or elsewhere who advocate integration for your children and send their own to private or public segregated schools; to those who defend or close their eyes to the livid stench of sadism, sex immorality and juvenile pregnancy infesting the mixed schools of the District of Columbia and elsewhere; to those who would overthrow the customs, morals and traditions of a way of life which has endured in honor and decency for centuries and embrace a new moral code prepared by nine men in Washington whose moral concepts they know nothing about; to those who would substitute strife, bitterness, turmoil and chaos for the tranquillity and happiness of an orderly society; to those who would destroy our way of life because of their pretended concern over what Soviet Russia may think of us—to all of these and their confederates, comrades and allies, [the frenzied Governor said] let me make it abundantly clear for the record now and hereafter, as governor of this state, I will not yield to that which I know to be wrong and will destroy every semblance of education for thousands of the children of Virginia.

(Almond's reference to the schools of the District of Columbia echoed the exaggerated 1956 report of the Davis Committee on conditions during the transition to unsegregated schools in Washington, D.C. In 1959, the District's integrated schools were operating with conspicuous success; juvenile delinquency had decreased and the educational level was higher than ever before. Governor Almond's lurid slander brought a quick protest from the Washington school authorities.)

Slamming the door against local option (which he himself was soon to propose), Almond said: "The grave constitutional crisis which has been thrust upon us makes it imperative that our energy, resources and efforts be launched and applied on a statewide basis."

In a momentary lapse into wisdom, the Governor announced his intention to appoint a commission "to formulate a sound and constructive program for submission to a special session of the General Assembly."

The *Richmond News Leader* reported the next day: "In his talk last night Almond removed any doubt that his administration might shift from the massive resistance stand."

Paying Almond one last compliment, Senator Byrd commented: "The notable speech of Governor Almond last night will further stiffen the resistance."

On the afternoon before the Governor's broadcast, a noisy demonstration by opponents of the funds-cut-off move of the Norfolk city council had forced a premature adjournment of a council meeting. The demonstration followed an impassioned speech by Mrs. Paul Schwartz, a P-TA representative, who said: "I am ashamed to say that I am a native of this city!"

Events moved swiftly now. Federal courts were in session almost daily to deal with the school cases of Arlington, Alexandria, Norfolk or Charlottesville. On Friday, January 23, Arlington County was ordered to admit four Negro pupils to Stratford Junior High School on February 2.

On Sunday, January 25, Almond issued a call for the General Assembly to meet in special session at noon the following Wednesday, January 28.

On Monday morning the manifesto of 100 Norfolk business and professional men appeared as a full-page newspaper advertisement. It said "the abandonment of our public school system is, in our opinion, unthinkable," and it urged the Norfolk city council to do "everything within its power to open all public schools as soon as possible." Signers of this statement included nine recipients of Norfolk's annual First Citizen award, two former mayors, together with leading bankers, industrialists, merchants, physicians and lawyers.

Also on Monday, Mayor Duckworth appeared in federal court to defend his plan for closing additional Norfolk schools; and the next day Judge Hoffman restrained the city council from engaging in any such "evasive scheme." The council bowed to this order, and it prepared to cooperate with the school board in the re-opening of the schools which had been closed. Resistance in this quarter came to an end.

President Eisenhower, commenting in a press conference on the Virginia situation, observed that "it comes down to the question of whether any citizen, either in official or civilian life, is ready to obey the laws of his state and his nation."

Almond seized this opportunity for one more retort in the full spirit of massive resistance.

The Virginia Supreme Court [he said] has never said or intimated that the violent transgressions of the United States Supreme Court on the Constitution are the law of the land. I am obeying, and will continue to obey, the laws of this state.

The special session was to open at noon on Wednesday, January 28. Negro children were scheduled to be admitted to white schools in at least two localities the following Monday, February 2.

The pressure upon the Governor for calling the special session had come almost entirely from the Defenders and other uncompromising segregationists, and Almond's own language had mounted to a new crescendo of defiance. It was generally expected now that he would offer the General Assembly some bold new proposal to prop the tottering structure of massive resistance.

The *Richmond Times-Dispatch* told its readers Wednesday morning:

"Virginia's General Assembly meets in emergency session at noon today to dig in for a last-ditch stand against racial integration of the public schools."

But Speaker Moore had doubts. The mild-mannered, russet-faced, sixty-two-year-old apple-grower who presided over the House of Delegates was a figure of singular significance in the story of massive resistance. For Moore was not only the hiking and vacation companion of Senator Byrd; he had become Byrd's most intimate confidant. Politicians in Richmond sometimes advised their fellows: "If you want to get the Byrd signal, watch Blackie Moore." Arriving in Richmond two days before the special session, Moore issued a carefully-worded statement. It was calculated either to hold Almond to massive resistance or to cause him the maximum embarrassment if he should flinch.

The Governor's action in calling the legislature together is good news [Moore said] because he has repeatedly stated he would not do so until he had an "effective" plan to meet the crisis which will face Virginia next week.

The legislature, I believe, stands ready to act promptly on any proposals by the Governor to prevent the integration of any of the schools anywhere in the state.

26. END OF AN ERA

When he addressed the General Assembly on Wednesday, January 28, 1959, it was Lindsay Almond's finest hour. Whatever may be said of his course up to that point, however much he may himself have contributed to the malevolent hysteria which prevailed, when the hard-pressed Governor called the legislature and the state back to sanity, he displayed a combination of courage, eloquence and skill which was admirable. He did what a leader in Arkansas, with whom his name had been unjustly coupled, has never dared to do. He set an example which to some extent many another Southern leader in time must follow.

The condemnation of the Supreme Court, the assertions of state sovereignty and insistence upon the evils of racial integration, which have become almost routine in political oratory in Virginia and the South, were all there; but they were not the burden of the Governor's speech. There was a minimum of flamboyance in his language, no oratorical flourishes in his delivery, never a quip and hardly a smile.

He stood in front of the Speaker's dais in the House of Delegates chamber, which was crowded with the influx of the state senators for the joint session. The galleries were packed to capacity. His old nemesis, Speaker Moore, looked down from the podium behind and watching intently out in front were Gray, Godwin, the younger Byrd, Boatwright, Thomson, all the stalwarts of the Byrd machine—also the anxious moderate contingent.

In a dark business suit, white shirt and gray tie, Almond was clad more conservatively than usual today. His florid face suggested controlled tension, as he clutched the lectern firmly with both hands and read slowly and clearly from his written text: "I am not aware of any crisis in the history of Virginia more grave, nor any emergency creating a more impelling necessity for the convening of the representatives of our people."

He outlined briefly the conflict with the federal government and the basic issues involved and came quickly to the point that further resistance would be futile.

It is not enough [the Governor said] for gentlemen to cry unto you and me, "Don't give up the ship!" "Stop them!" "It must not happen," or "It can be prevented." If any of them knows the way through the dark maze of judicial aberration and constitutional exploitation, I call upon them to shed the light for which Virginia stands in dire need in this her dark and agonizing hour. No fairminded person would be so unreasonable as to seek to hold me responsible for failure to exercise powers which the state is powerless to bestow.

Almond reviewed his own long efforts, beginning as attorney general in 1953, and the efforts of the General Assembly, "to maintain Virginia's rights and save her public school system." He said that the laws enacted to this end "have been stricken down by a federal court and by the Supreme Court of Appeals of Virginia."

Referring to "those who insist that I invoke the police power of this state," the Governor said that, if necessity should arise, he could, and would, invoke the police power to preserve order. But, he declared,

The police power cannot be asserted to thwart or override the decree of a court of competent jurisdiction, state or federal. . . .

There are those who insist that I seek authority from the General Assembly to padlock and police any school threatened with the imminence of integration. The Assembly cannot confer such authority.

I am willing to serve in durance vile with those who give advice, if it will accomplish the desired purpose. I know of nothing more futile than a penal sentence that contributes to nothing but the ridiculous.

. . . It should be clearly understood that the governor, the attorney general, and any other officer of the state, is as amenable to suit as any other citizen when he seeks to perform an unlawful act, or to do some unconstitutional thing under the guise and cloak that it is an act of the state and not of the individual.

Contrary to the opinion of some, I cannot conceive how the Pupil Placement Act can be asserted either as a buffer or a bulwark between the overriding and superior power of the federal government and the operation of a segregated school. That which the state is powerless to do it cannot confer upon an administrative agency.

The Governor referred to the commission which he had already announced his intention to appoint, and listed eleven phases of the school problem which he would submit to it for study. In the meantime he asked the legislature to enact a tuition grant plan independent of public school appropriations and without reference to the race problem (thus free from the constitutional objections raised by the State Supreme Court of Appeals), repeal the compulsory school attendance law, and pass a law against bombing threats. He wished the legislators to take these three steps, and go home.

Almond was anxious above all to prevent any new legislative excesses. He said:

I most respectfully and earnestly recommend that the Assembly not undertake at this time to deal with the complexities involved in the formulation of the program outlined.

I recommend that the Assembly promptly enact the emergency measures which I shall submit, and then stand in recess to receive further recommendations following the study and report by the commission. . . .

There was only mild applause. It came at a complimentary reference to Attorney General Harrison and at the more belligerent passages here and there. The full significance of his speech sank in slowly. Moderates conferred with one another, first incredulously, then with deep relief. Some were jubilant. Some Byrd machine leaders were silent or commented that the Governor had not gone far enough, but many of that famous organization shared at first in the generally favorable reaction. Almond had won the day.

A poll was promptly conducted by telephone by newspapers in Richmond, Norfolk, Arlington, Roanoke and Lynchburg.

More than two out of three citizens questioned expressed approval of Almond's new approach to the school problem. The question was: "How were you impressed in general, by Governor Almond's message to the Legislature?" To this 67 per cent replied "favorably," 17 per cent "Unfavorably," and 16 per cent "Undecided." Approximately the same majority thought that the Governor should not have recommended any other course.

The Governor dominated the brief special session in all but one particular, which he did not emphasize. He wanted the legislators to adopt the three measures which he had recommended, and go home Saturday. His bills were passed on time and with near unanimity. A handful objected only to repeal of the compulsory school attendance law. But the legislature insisted upon staying in session through Monday. The school boards of Arlington and Norfolk had announced that schools would be integrated Monday in accordance with court orders, and a majority of members thought they should be on hand "just in case."

A series of proposals were made by bitter-end segregationists. Gray had a scheme for placing the whole normal public school appropriation in a tuition grant fund and empowering the Governor to transfer funds only to segregated public schools. Proposals were made: to close all public schools temporarily; to have the General Assembly itself take full charge of all public school operation; to make it a felony for any public school administrator to enroll a child not assigned to the school by the Pupil Placement Board; and to require referendum approval by the voters of the community before any closed public school was re-opened. Segregationist Delegate Frank P. Moncure introduced a bill to close all public schools until they could be inspected for fire hazards!

Against all these schemes, the Governor stood like a stone wall. Behind his labors of persuasion in conference lay the threat of his veto, and a now clear-cut Almond faction fought the proposals in committee and on the floor. The proposals were resoundingly defeated. Only a joint resolution reiterating the Assembly's opposition to school integration—which many moderates considered harmless—passed both houses. State Senator Haddock, however, who cast the lone dissenting vote on this resolution in the Senate, issued a statement afterward, saying that it seemed inappropriate to subscribe to a document "expressing further bitterness of feeling. Such things as this," he said, "have helped to build tension in our state to fever pitch within the past four years."

In Charlottesville, a series of events had occurred which eliminated that city from the area of immediate crisis. The Charlottesville school board, in a meeting on January 26, voted to re-open the schools which had been closed and integrate them, when required by federal court orders. The city council the following day unanimously endorsed the school board's action, noting that "some integration must result," either now or in September, depending on the outcome of a request for stay of the district court order. The Fourth Circuit Court of Appeals was impressed. Judge Simon Soboloff termed Charlottesville's course "an historic event. . . . For the first time," he said, "a town in Virginia has set the pace by saying, 'We're through with resistance.' " "Satisfied of the defendants' good faith," Judge Soboloff issued a stay of the district court order until the beginning of the next school term in September.

The 1,200-name petition for open schools in Charlottesville appeared in the press on January 31, belatedly, but in time still to be of value in strengthening public sentiment for the operation of public schools in accordance with the law of the land.

In Warren County legal action for the re-opening of the high school remained to be taken.

In Norfolk, when it was finally clear that the closed schools would be re-opened and integrated, the hitherto obstructionist city council called upon the people of Norfolk to conduct themselves in a peaceful and law-abiding manner.

"No violence or other unlawful action will be tolerated," the council warned. "The city's law enforcement agencies have been alerted to preserve and protect the property, peace and safety of the city and all its inhabitants."

From Arlington, David L. Krupsaw, county board chairman, wired Governor Almond on Sunday:

Arlington appreciates your courageous leadership and your realistic approach to Virginia's school problems. We assure you that Arlington County officials, in accordance with your wishes, have taken every step necessary to make our school opening tomorrow quiet and orderly.

Though Arlington County was overwhelmingly opposed to closing schools to prevent integration, its segregationist minority had been active and its small Defenders organization was exceptionally aggressive. The latter had circularized the 1,070 white pupils of Stratford Junior High School, urging them to stay away from school and offering anti-integration signs to be used in picketing. But members of interracial groups, P-TA's and other civic organizations had been more effective than they in preparing Stratford pupils for the event. Both white and Negro pupils in the classes to be integrated had been sympathetically coached; they had even been given opportunities to get acquainted with their prospective classmates.

Virginians throughout the state sat by their radios Monday morning. Some, after listening to predictions of "strife, bitterness, chaos and confusion," waited for the riots to begin. In

Richmond massive resisters had held the legislature in session to be ready for emergency action.

Then the reports began to come through. From Arlington an announcer said: "The colored children have entered the school and the white children are making friends with them."

From Norfolk reports came that the Negro children had all entered their schools in an orderly manner.

There was little more to report—no crowds, no disorder. The tranquillity was devastating!

It was a melancholy day for the battered massive resistance bloc in the General Assembly. One member deplored "the rape of our constitutional rights." Said another: "The most distressing thing we have witnessed is another step in the breakdown of our constitutional form of government. . . ." Delegate Pope mourned "one of the blackest days Virginia has faced since reconstruction. . . ." Delegate Carneal called it "a day of infamy." Delegate Thomson sighed: "There's a sickness in my heart."

They did not wish to adjourn the legislature without making one last effort. An abortive attempt was made in the state Senate to revive massive resistance by a bill which would require the Governor to close any school which did not meet the bill's definition of "efficient," which, in its circuitous language, could only mean "segregated." The bill was defeated by a vote of seventeen to twenty-two, with one moderate Senator absent.

At 6:14 P.M., a Senate-House committee called upon the Governor to notify him that the Assembly was ready to adjourn, and to receive any further communication. Almond, chatting with his office staff, jumped up to meet the committee with a grin. He smoked cigarettes at times of tension; he was smoking a friendly pipe now.

"You certainly do have a big smile on your face," said Delegate John Cooke, the House floor leader.

"Yes, John," the Governor said, "I certainly do, thank you. Thank you, every one, and God bless every one of you. You have been just wonderful."

27. NO STRIFE

IF WE were concerned only with the dramatic quality of this story, this is where the curtain should fall. When twenty-one Negro children trudged shyly into Arlington and Norfolk white schools, the ninety-year era of race segregation in Virginia's public schools, and the state's four years of resistance to federal authority, came to an end.

There would be more litigation, some further sensations and many more fulminations. The progressive implementation of the Supreme Court's desegregation ruling would be slow and reluctant. Politicians would still call themselves "massive resisters." They would form a "massive resistance bloc" in the legislature, and talk irresponsibly to constituents about bringing massive resistance back. The "betrayers" would be unceasingly denounced. But the page had been turned and history had moved on. All the king's horses and all the king's men could never put massive resistance back together again.

However, items of unfinished business remain—like the school desegregation cases of Alexandria, Warren, Charlottesville and Prince Edward. The reader will also wish to know what the legislature did in subsequent sessions and the impact of it all upon the Byrd machine, upon that very human individual who is the central figure in this drama, Lindsay Almond —and upon the rest of the South.

First, we should take a closer look at the surprisingly peaceful manner in which the Arlington and Norfolk schools were integrated. Police authorities in neither of those cities had quite shared the qualms of Virginia extremists—or of national observers, as represented by the heavy contingents of newspaper, radio and television men on hand. But plans made long in advance were carried out in a thoroughgoing manner and no possibility of violence was overlooked.

The methods of the two police departments differed in one important respect. In Arlington, approximately 100 police officers assigned to the school area were in full uniform and carried heavy nightsticks, gas masks and riot guns; in Norfolk, most of the police were in plain clothes. Both methods were completely successful.

By way of notifying fanatics in any part of the sprawling urban county that no disturbance would be tolerated, Arlington police, in blue uniforms and white helmets, lined up before dawn in eight-man squads on the court-house square. Squad leaders, carrying walkie-talkie radios, marched them to police wagons and automobiles, which took them to the Stratford Junior High School, situated in a residential area. There they lined the street approaches to the school, where parking was prohibited. Fourteen officers and a policewoman, in plain clothes, were stationed inside the school.

In Norfolk, on the other hand, with its dense population and more widespread race tension, the police were anxious to avoid spectacular operations and show of force. Each of the six schools to be integrated was patrolled by plain clothes men. Policemen in plain clothes also kept an eye on the homes of the Negro pupils who were entering white schools in case hoodlums should attempt reprisals. Uniformed officers were in readiness in case they should be needed.

No crowds gathered in either Arlington or Norfolk—except the swarm of newspaper, radio and camera men.

Entering the seventh grade at Arlington's Stratford Junior High School were four twelve-year-old Negro children, Gloria Thompson and three boys, Ronald Deskins, Lance D. Newman and Michael G. Jones. They gathered in the morning at the two-bedroom apartment of the Deskins and were driven to school in one car, with parents of three of them. As they walked to the side door of the building for their first class, they said a polite "Good morning," to the policemen stationed along the way.

The Negro children in the Arlington school were not isolated, or shunned, either in their classrooms or in the school cafeteria. They took part in class discussions and chatted with the white children during recesses. They ate at the same table with white pupils. School teachers present reported that the white children seemed to be more interested in the police officers having their lunch nearby than in the presence of the Negroes.

Three of the school's 1,070 pupils arrived at the school and left because of the Negroes; telephone inquiries later revealed that the parents of two more were keeping their children out of school for the same reason. Nevertheless, the total of seventy-three pupils absent Monday was less than the usual absenteeism rate of 7 per cent, and the highest attendance grade was the integrated seventh. Superintendent Ray E. Reid said that the parents of many absent students called the school office in the morning to assure authorities that their absence was due to illness.

In Norfolk seventeen Negro pupils were admitted to six white high schools, and the white pupils paid little attention to them. No open insults were reported; private expressions of antagonism were few. After dismissal at Norview High School, a small group of white students clustered around a newsreel cameraman, chanted: "Two-four-six-eight, we don't want to integrate!" But other students pointed to these contemptuously as trouble-makers.

The Negroes being integrated in Norfolk were older than those in Arlington. They arrived at school in ones and twos. Lewis Cousins, the only Negro to enter Maury High School, was to find himself later a segregationist exhibit. Lewis walked early into the auditorium and sat in the front row, near the middle, while pupils were being assigned to classes. A striking press photograph caught the Negro boy sitting in a hall half a dozen seats from any white pupil. The picture was widely cited as an illustration of the ostracism and loneliness of Negro pupils in predominantly white schools.

Only 6,400 pupils returned to the reopened schools in Norfolk on Monday out of a total enrollment of approximately 10,000. The situation was complicated there by the fact that the schools had been closed for five months and a variety of private school arrangements had been made.

Police precautions in both Arlington and Norfolk were relaxed in a few days. By the end of the week enrollment in the re-opened Norfolk schools had risen to 6,868—of whom 1,856 had been without any schooling whatever from the September closing until the public school re-opening.

Meanwhile the Alexandria school board had received a desegregation order. It had been told to admit nine Negro pupils to a white high school and two white elementary schools. By the end of the week requests for a stay of the order had been rejected, by the federal district court first and then by the Fourth Circuit Court of Appeals. On Tuesday, February 10, the nine Negro children entered white schools in an atmosphere of complete tranquillity and order. The Alexandria in-

cident passed almost unnoticed. It received only minor headlines in the Virginia press.

28. THE "BOYCOTT" IN WARREN

THE SCHOOL problem in Charlottesville and Warren County
differed radically from that in Arlington, Alexandria and Norfolk. In Arlington and Alexandria it was a matter of admitting
Negro children to white schools which had been in normal
operation since the beginning of the school term. In the other
three areas schools had been closed. In Norfolk a majority of
the displaced pupils had been able to make only unsatisfactory
schooling arrangements or none at all.

In Charlottesville and Warren, virtually all the displaced
pupils had been accommodated in some way. Most of them
were attending private classes which were temporarily satisfactory. In Charlottesville, nonetheless, when a federal court
order permitted desegregation to be postponed until the following September and the two schools re-opened, nearly all
of the pupils returned, amid general rejoicing. The three
emergency private school programs were discontinued. Following a plan approved by the court, the twelve Negro children seeking enrollment in white schools were not required to
return to their segregated schools but were furnished special
tutoring in school board offices.

Warren County's situation was unlike any of the rest. In this
county, where immediate desegregation was insisted upon, the
private school improvisation had been achieved with consider-

able enthusiasm and community effort. Many were resigned to this private school as a permanent substitute for a racially integrated public high school. Many others, who opposed it in principle and deplored the closing of the public high school, were unwilling to have their children's schooling interrupted by another change during the same school year. It was not even a matter of changing at mid-term; the second semester was already under way. Sentiment was virtually unanimous for continuing the private school program until the end of the year. Since later events were to be widely interpreted as a unanimous decision on the part of the white people of Warren County to abandon their public high school rather than accept racial integration, it behooves us to examine those events and give their background in some detail.

On a motion filed by an attorney for the Negro plaintiffs on February 6, Federal District Judge John Paul on February 10 ordered the county to re-open its public high school and admit the twenty-two Negro applicants the following week. He rejected a plea of the Warren County school board for permission to postpone the re-opening until September. His decision was appealed to the Fourth Circuit Court of Appeals, and that court confirmed the lower court order to re-open the school. In the hearing before the court of appeals on the sixteenth the attorney for the school board, William J. Phillips, said:

I feel the people of Warren County are 100 per cent behind the attitude of the school board. It would be a tremendous effort to reopen the high school. Maybe some would come back. But it's the concensus of 98 per cent of the people that they feel the children's schooling shouldn't be interrupted now.

Nevertheless, Judge Sobeloff said at the conclusion of the hearing: "I think by any standard that what Warren County has been doing is indefensible. . . . I have heard nothing that would justify altering the lower court's ruling."

While the case was pending on appeal approximately 1,000 citizens gathered in a mass meeting in Front Royal and by an almost unanimous vote adopted a resolution, saying that it would be best for the pupils to continue their studies without interruption and requesting the Warren County Educational Foundation to continue its private school program. School board attorney Phillips, who addressed the meeting, said he intended "to give Judge Sobeloff assurance that we will comply with the order" in September; but he said he would ask that the board be allowed to keep the public high school closed until then, because, he said, "it isn't a question of integration or of segregation, but . . . the greatest good to the greatest number."

Four days later the Warren County Educational Foundation announced the results of a poll of the parents of the 763 pupils in its private school. Out of 587 who had returned the questionnaires, 582 said they preferred to keep their children in the private school for the remainder of the school term.

School Superintendent Q. D. Gasque announced that the enrollment of students who wished to return to Warren High School would begin Wednesday morning, February 18, at nine o'clock. The Warren County Educational Foundation announced that it would continue its private school program until June. Duncan C. Gibbs, president of the foundation, said it had enough money, $120,000, to operate until June without charging tuition. He added that the private school's thirty-one teachers, twenty-six of whom had formerly taught in the public high school, had voted unanimously to continue working for the foundation.

At a meeting of the school board Tuesday evening, Superintendent Gasque said: "There is very little we can do until Wednesday, as I don't know how many pupils we will have at the high school." At most, observers expected only a few dozen white pupils to return.

Wednesday came and no white children returned. No white child applied for enrollment in the Warren County High School. Only the twenty-two Negro applicants enrolled. Superintendent Gasque said: "My guess is that parents of children in the private schools don't wish to interrupt the studies of their children another time this year."

There was no disorder in Front Royal which directly concerned any of the twenty-two Negro children when they entered the high school, but one incident among white onlookers required the attention of the police. A small group of townspeople gathered around sixty-five-year-old John G. Bowman, a former bus driver for the county schools, who was voicing strong anti-segregation views to newspaper reporters. "Segregation is wrong," Bowman said, "politically, economically, socially—from every angle."

Someone cried: "Speak for yourself." Another warned: "I'd be afraid to go to bed tonight if I were you."

Before police dispersed the crowd, Bowman said that when the public high school closed, he had sent his two children, who were formerly enrolled there, to school in Rappahannock County. They would remain in Rappahannock for the remainder of the school term, "because," he said, "they don't want to come back after the middle of the year."

Mrs. Parke Wagner, ninth grade English teacher in the private school, said:

We're not boycotting the school. We're not going up there, simply because we're convinced that it is for the welfare of the youngsters not to be disrupted again this year. If those kids had no private school, they would have gone to the public school today. I'd like to think that we'll all be together at the high school next year.

The "boycott" of the public high school made newspaper headlines across the nation. To many in the South the people of Warren County became heroes overnight. Pictured by cartoonists as a soldier holding the Confederate banner, the little county was said to have stood "like a stone wall" against racial integration.

The *Richmond Times-Dispatch*, whose reporters had given a full and true account of events in Warren County, said editorially nonetheless:

In the gloomy annals of the five-year constitutional crisis, Warren's stonewall refusal to surrender, will remain a bright spot remembered.

The people of Warren peacefully re-opened their high school to the children of colored citizens—as ordered by the court.

But they refused, as Virginians, to send their children to a federally dominated school.

The unanimity of the "Warren court" was thus matched by the unanimity of Warren County.

Senator James O. Eastland, of Mississippi, said on the floor of the United States Senate that the white students of Warren County, who refused to return to an integrated school, were an "inspiration to all the South to stand steadfast under the lash of federal court tyranny."

The Alabama legislature by unanimous vote adopted a resolution, saying:

Whereas freedom of choice in association by individuals or groups is a fundamental, inalienable right, which is being exercised in Warren County, Virginia, where the white residents of that county have set such a fine example for the South in refusing to return to a public high school, re-opened on an integrated basis under a federal court order; and. . .

Whereas the people of Warren County have furnished an inspired example for all the people of the South; now therefore

Be it resolved by the Legislature of Alabama, both Houses concurring, that this body expresses to the people of Warren County, Virginia, its feeling of deep admiration for their splendid conduct, and warmly commends them for their allegiance to principle and for this bold and courageous action.

Warren remained a symbol of Southern resistance, and of nostalgic Confederate glory, until white children in substantial number duly returned to the Warren county high school in September. Senator Strom Thurmond, of South Carolina, visited Front Royal in June, apppropriately, to dedicate a Confederate museum. His address was largely devoted to the "courage and determination shown here in 1959."

Your example [the Senator said] removed any doubt as to whether Virginians still retained the spirit and love of principle demonstrated so inspiringly in the 1860's. . . . Truly, my fellow citizens, by your calm determination, your sacrifice, you have made Front Royal the very symbol of the South's determination to preserve and maintain states' rights.

29. DEBACLE IN PRINCE EDWARD

ON MAY 5, 1959, the Fourth Circuit Court of Appeals upset the mild ruling of Judge Hutcheson in the case of Prince Edward County. The appeals court noted that 1965 had been fixed as a tentative deadline for desegregation of that county's schools, "because the judge was of the opinion that the school board should have ten years from the second decision of the Supreme Court in *Brown* v. *Board of Education* on May 31, 1955. . . ."

But the appeals court observed:

Other communities in the state have taken steps to meet the problem and solve it, whereas in Prince Edward County the school authorities have taken no effective action whatever during the four years since the second decision in *Brown* v. *Board of Education* was rendered, and even today contemplate no action in the future. . . .

It directed the district court to order the Prince Edward school board "to take immediate steps in this regard to the end that the applications be considered so as to permit the entrance of qualified persons into the white schools in the school term beginning September, 1959." The original suit was on behalf of high school pupils only. The court said that the school board should be required also "to make plans for the admission of pupils in the elementary schools of the county without regard to race and to receive and consider applications to this end at the earliest practical date."

Actually orders were not issued by the district court until nearly a year later; and no Negro pupil applied for admission to any white school in Prince Edward County. Judge Hutcheson said he would implement the order of the higher court whenever attorneys for the plaintiffs so requested. But he was spared this painful duty. The NAACP attorneys did not request further court action in the case, and Judge Hutcheson retired from the bench four months later.

Nevertheless, the appeals court decision was taken in Prince Edward County as the signal for the long-contemplated abandonment of public schools. Blanton Hanbury, president of the Prince Edward Educational Corporation, announced the day after the decision was delivered that the corporation expected to have "everything in shape" for private schooling by September. His organization had over $12,000 in cash on hand and expected to update expired pledges for $200,000 more.

On June 26 the board of supervisors adopted a budget that included nothing for the operation of public schools. Anxious to avoid any connection of public funds with private schools, the supervisors refused even to provide for the tuition grants, a part of the cost of which was available from the state. Ironically, the only money allotted for schools was $30,500 for debt service on the money which had been borrowed to build the new Negro high school. At the same meeting the board cut the tax rate 53 per cent, the proportion normally destined for public schools. Thus public education came to an end in Prince Edward County.

Under national radio-television spotlight, the private school organization staged a formal opening on September 10. Few adults entered the motion picture theater where the ceremonies were held, but many townspeople gathered around the radio in business places on Main Street to listen. Approximately 400 high school students jammed the theater, where they heard foundation president Hanbury, Roy R. Pearson, school administrator, and Farmville Mayor William F. Watkins urge the pupils to do their best work. Pearson, a retired oil company executive, had resigned as chairman of the county school board to undertake this task.

"You must remember this year," Hanbury said, "that the spotlight of publicity on a national basis will be on you and your accomplishment."

Invoking God's blessing on the undertaking, the Rev. Lloyd Arehart, pastor of the Farmville Presbyterian Church, said:

"We pray, not only for these, but for all those young people both white and Negro, who may be bereft of educational opportunities today. Grant that these opportunities may speedily be renewed under Thy holy will. . . ."

The following Monday, September 14, the private school

classes began. They were in two high schools (called "upper academies"), and in six grade schools (called "lower academies") in sixteen buildings scattered over the county. In rural areas, classes met in the Sunday School departments of churches; in Farmville, churches, stores, a former blacksmith shop and private homes were used. Sixty-six teachers were employed, most of them from the closed public schools, receiving the same salaries as before.

Transportation was afforded by fourteen buses, purchased as surplus from other counties by a separate organization, called "Patrons, Inc." The Prince Edward Educational Foundation steered clear of anything that might involve public tax money. Typewriters for the business education classes were rented, although typewriters were sitting idle in the closed Farmville High School; library books in the public high school's library were not used, although many of them had been donated by private individuals; and, of course, state tuition grants were refused. A plea for book donations brought in some 10,000 volumes for the private school library.

The enrollment in the private schools was 1,475 out of a former white public school enrollment of 1,562. About half of the foundation's budget of $310,000 had now been raised in cash. Taxpayers were expected to contribute the amount of their tax savings, since the county's levy for schools had been repealed.

"No Trespassing" signs were tacked on the walls of the county's twenty-two public schools.

The over 1,700 Negro children of school age was left entirely without schools. Fifty Negro juniors and seniors were later sent to the high school division of Kittrell College, a Negro Methodist institution in North Carolina. They were given $150 scholarships by Kittrell, and the Negro Prince Ed-

152 VIRGINIA'S MASSIVE RESISTANCE

ward County Christian Association undertook to raise money
to cover the remainder of their expenses at the rate of $210
each.

On October 12, the Supreme Court refused to review the
decision of the Fourth Circuit Court of Appeals which had required prompt desegregation of Prince Edward County's
public schools.

In December a group of white citizens set up an organization called "Southside Schools, Inc.," which undertook to
provide segregated private schooling for the Negro children.
Although the foundation for white private schools had rejected governmental tuition grants as possibly weakening its
legal position, Southside Schools, Inc. decided to take the risk
in the matter of schooling for Negroes. It fixed a tuition
charge for each child of $240, the amount of the tuition grant
which might be available from public funds. The move received considerable publicity and an application form was
sent to the parents of each of the 1,700 Negro children.

But NAACP leaders condemned this initiative as "trying to
entice you away from your rights." NAACP attorney Oliver
Hill said to Prince Edward's schoolless Negro pupils: "All you
are losing now is one or two years of basic education, but, if
you succeed you'll get far more than you ever would in Jim
Crow schools."

Only one of the county's 1,700 Negro children applied for
enrollment in this project. The board of directors of Southside
Schools, Inc. gave up plans for beginning operations in February, 1960, but issued a statement which said in part:

It is apparent that there will be no public schools in the county
within the foreseeable future due to the court order entered against
the Prince Edward School Board. . . .
Feeling, as we do, that it is necessary and important that all
children of this county be afforded an opportunity to secure an

education, we are proceeding toward our objectives and we intend
to establish detailed plans for the operation of a system of schools
throughout Prince Edward County for the school session of 1960–
61.

Meanwhile, Negro leaders announced plans and set about
raising a fund of $16,500, to operate ten "training centers" for
Negro children, which would provide a recreation program
and some instruction in such basic subjects as reading and
arithmetic.

In the fall of 1960 Prince Edward County moved into another year with only makeshift private schools for white children and no schools for Negroes. The county's governing
board had decided now to risk a policy of indirect government
aid to the financially hard-pressed private schools. It accepted
the state "scholarship" grant of $125 per pupil and allocated
an additional $100 per pupil from county funds. It added to
this a grant of $35 per pupil for transportation in the case of
children residing more than half a mile from their schools. It
provided further, under new state legislation, that donations
to the private schools would be credited on real estate and
personal property taxes up to 25 per cent of the taxpayer's
bill. But the schools situation in Prince Edward remained an
open sore.

In June NAACP attorneys had initiated a legal effort to get
a federal court order enjoining officials from refusing to
operate public schools in that county. The action took the
form of a supplemental complaint to the original Prince
Edward County case, but the State Board of Education, the
state superintendent of public instruction and the Prince
Edward board of supervisors were brought in as defendants
in addition to the local school board. The NAACP attorneys
based their argument on the requirement in the Virginia Constitution for the maintenance of public schools and on the

Fourteenth Amendment of the United States Constitution. Prince Edward and state officials in their reply, filed in October, contended that the complaint should have been brought first to a state court, that the federal court order prohibiting race discrimination in public schools does not require that schools be operated and that appropriating money for schools is a legislative prerogative, not subject to court order.

On December 5 a group of Negro leaders presented a petition to the Prince Edward board of supervisors, requesting that public schools be re-opened and adding: "If we fail in this appeal, and if you refuse our respectful petition, we are prepared to use all nonviolent means to achieve our purpose. . . ." It was clearly indicated that pressure might include a boycott of white merchants.

Business in Prince Edward was already bad, and a number of families, both white and colored, had left the county. Among white residents, openly expressed dissent was still rare, but as 1960 ended there was increasing evidence that many would welcome a court order bringing the dismal experiment to an end.

30. INTEGRATION AND PRIVATE SCHOOLS IN 1959–1960

IN CONTRAST to the melancholy developments in Prince Edward County, the beginnings of desegregation elsewhere in Virginia moved smoothly, without any interruption in public school operation and without disturbance.

In Warren County the myth of a "unanimous boycott" was

dispelled at the beginning of the regular school term. Despite strong competition from the now popular private school establishment, 417 white pupils, along with nineteen Negroes, enrolled in September in the Warren County high school.

In Charlottesville, twelve Negro children enrolled in September, along with 1,200 whites, in the two schools which had been closed the previous September. The segregated private schools of the Charlottesville Educational Foundation, laboring under financial discouragements and some administrative dissension, operated throughout the year with an enrollment of approximately 540.

In Norfolk where seventeen Negroes were enrolled in six formerly all-white schools in the spring, desegregation was extended in September, 1959, to one elementary school, and five more Negro children were attending integrated schools. A total of approximately 12,000 Norfolk children were now in racially mixed schools. Less than 300 had taken state "scholarships" to attend private schools, about 200 of these being pupils of the new segregationist Tidewater Academy.

In Arlington County, where integration in the spring had been limited to four Negro children in Stratford Junior High School, new federal court orders extended desegregation in September, 1959, to an additional high school and an elementary school, and nineteen more Negroes were now in integrated schools. In February, 1960, seven more Negro children were admitted to predominantly white schools in Alexandria; and, climaxing a new litigation, fourteen were admitted to two white high schools in Floyd County. In these three localities no movement to set up any private school escape developed and attendance was not appreciably affected by the presence of Negro children in previously all-white public schools.

In Floyd County, the first locality in Southwest Virginia to desegregate public schools, the operation was carried out with extraordinary ease. Only 4.6 per cent of the 10,786 people of this mountainous county are colored, and it had no Negro high school. As in Warren County, Negro pupils had been transported to a high school in a neighboring county, a distance of about thirty-five miles each way.

The *Roanoke World-News* commented on the Floyd County incident as follows:

The quiet, orderly, almost unostentatious manner in which 13 Negro children were integrated into white high schools of Floyd County yesterday is a credit to all concerned—pupils, parents and teachers. . . .

Guided by the Floyd school board and Superintendent of Schools James H. Combs, everyone in the county appeared to have made a conscious effort to prepare for the inevitable since Judge Roby C. Thompson's order was handed down last September. It was generally recognized that abolishment of all public schools to avoid integration simply didn't make sense.

And so there began a period of training and preparation on the part of white pupils that is without parallel in this state. The result was that boys and girls behaved with exemplary reserve and caution. Neither was there any demonstration of protest or resentment by their elders. . . .

What happened at Floyd and Check High Schools yesterday is certain to be repeated eventually in many other counties of Southwest Virginia. When the time comes, we feel confident they will meet the decision with the same calm and good sense shown by Floyd County people yesterday.

In the matter of social activities in the integrated public schools in Virginia, school authorities ceased officially to sponsor any dance or other social function, but groups of parents and pupils were allowed to use school premises for such activities among invited, and segregated, groups. The Arlington school board announced that school facilities would be rented at six dollars an evening to "responsible adult groups sponsoring non-integrated social events similar to those held last year and limited to students of the school and their dates."

It is worthy of note that no new private schools were set up in Virginia except in districts where public schools were actually closed. The regular, long-established private schools expanded their facilities during the year only, by a classroom here and a classroom there, to accommodate less than 200 more pupils than their previous enrollment. The increase in truancy in the state resulting from repeal of the state compulsory school attendance law was slight; twenty-six localities had returned to compulsory attendance by local ordinance.

Some of the private schools which had been set up in schoolless emergencies continued to function. New private schools in Warren and Charlottesville and the small segregationist academy in Norfolk made plans, or took steps, to acquire real estate and gave evidence of becoming more or less permanent institutions. In Prince Edward, where the public schools had closed only in September, 1959, the white people contemplated relying upon their elaborate system of private schools for the foreseeable future. The new private high schools were called "academies" and took such names as: Mosby Academy, in Front Royal; Rock Hill Academy, in Charlottesville; Prince Edward Academy, in Prince Edward; and Tidewater Academy, in Norfolk.

That factors other than indigenous race prejudice affected the pattern of development of the new private schools is indicated by the fact that only the private school in Warren County, the district with the lowest percentage of Negroes in its population (8 per cent), rivaled the public school in attendance. In Warren, 435 children were enrolled in Mosby Academy, while only an approximately equal number attended Warren County high school. Warren, which had made sensational news as the scene of the first school-closing and again of the so-called "boycott," had been a center of unique agitation.

Its martyrdom and its dubious glory as a bulwark of state rights, and pride in the private school, which it had with great civic zeal established, contributed to the reluctance of Warren citizens to abandon the undertaking.

The Warren local of the Textile Workers Union of America, Mosby Academy's heaviest financial backer, ran into trouble in the spring of 1960 with the union's national headquarters. The latter, which had frowned upon its segregationist activity from the beginning, moved in when the local voted to buy $8,000 of bonds to help finance new private school construction. On the ground that this was an improper use of union funds, the local's officers were removed and its assets were frozen. Individual members, however, continued to aid the private school foundation, and substantial contributions were received by it from other sources. The school's operating cost was now largely met from tuition fees at the rate of $220 per pupil, this amount having now been established as the "scholarship" grant in that county. Mosby Academy was going forward with plans for a twenty-two-classroom, $250,000 building, and seemed eminently a going concern.

The plan for aiding private schooling with public funds by means of "scholarships" had tended to soften the psychological blow of public school integration among strongly segregationist elements. To the new private schools of Warren, Charlottesville and Norfolk it was a practical and almost indispensable boon. But the "scholarships" were now generously available, without reference to race segregation, to all who wished to attend qualified non-sectarian private schools.

Much of the state's "scholarship" money was being distributed among private school pupils not immediately concerned with the matter of race segregation. Many parents whose children had long attended private schools were glad to accept this contribution from public funds toward the cost of their children's education. Some children were actually using their Virginia "scholarship" payments to attend out-of-state schools which were racially integrated. A survey made by the *Richmond News Leader* in November, 1959, revealed that a total of 1,820 "scholarships" had been granted under the state's revised plan. Of these, only 1,283 were distributed in the partially integrated school districts of Alexandria, Arlington, Charlottesville, Norfolk and Warren. (No "scholarships" were requested in Prince Edward.) In the integrated school district of Alexandria only thirty-two "scholarships" had been granted; but in the populous adjoining county of Fairfax 263 private school pupils were receiving this form of state aid. There were no integrated public schools in Fairfax, but it was a common practice among well-to-do families in that county to send their children to private schools.

Sixteen Virginia public schools were now integrated. Allowing for occasional drop-outs, the total number of Negro children in integrated public schools in Virginia increased from thirty in the spring of 1959 to eighty-six in September and 103 in February, 1960. The state which summoned the South to massive resistance was moving—at a snail's pace, to be sure—but somewhat faster than any other strictly Southern state in complying with the Supreme Court's ruling.

Public school desegregation began in the fall in the additional school districts of Richmond, Roanoke and Galax and Fairfax and Pulaski counties, bringing the total of integrated schools in Virginia to thirty-seven in eleven localities. The number of Negro children in integrated schools was now 208. The progress of desegregation was still peaceful. At the end of 1960 no instance of violence or of public disorder related to school desegregation had been reported in Virginia.

31. WHAT THEY DID TO ALMOND

THE GOVERNOR'S acceptance of the inevitable and the collapse of massive resistance, as January, 1959, ended and February began, had aroused vociferous resentment in Southside Virginia and among the extremists of the Defenders of State Sovereignty and Individual Liberties everywhere. The members of the hard core of the Byrd machine were bitter, but they were inclined for the most part to bide their time.

As Sussex County Clerk William B. Cocke said, many in Southside Virginia had felt little concern at the calling of the legislature into session, "because they thought they had a champion of their cause." Now the feeling was: "We've been betrayed." But there were some responsible leaders even in the Fourth District who agreed with Lunenburg County Clerk J. T. Waddell, Jr., that the Governor "probably did all that was legally possible." There was also disaffection in the ranks of the Defenders. Attendance at Defenders rallies in February and March fell far below announced expectations, and, although that group was to initiate one spectacular demonstration, its influence in the state as a whole began a steady decline.

The demonstration was staged by a special organization, called the "Bill of Rights Crusade," which Defenders leaders had set in motion early in February. On March 31, the opening day of the reconvened legislative session, approximately five thousand angry Virginians, mainly from the Southside, assembled in front of the Capitol in Richmond. There they listened and roared with applause while Edward J. Silverman, a handsome young advertising salesman from a small Fourth District town, with astonishing oratorical talent, called on the legislature to "regain the leadership" which had been "so shamefully surrendered in recent weeks."

Silverman remarked sneeringly that the Governor "did not see fit to accept our invitation to be with us." Almond did not, indeed, appear. But practically all the members of the General Assembly sat on the steps of the south portico to watch the show and hear the speech. Some were amused, some were embarrassed, some approved. Most of them (but not Speaker Moore) refrained from joining in the applause of the throng.

The Commission on Education, as the body which the Governor set up to formulate a new program was called, had labored through most of February and March. Its chairman was State Senator Mosby G. Perrow, Jr., a quietly efficient legislator, long identified with the Byrd organization, who had followed an inconspicuously moderate course during the desegregation crisis. The Commission held public hearings and received petitions and advice from many quarters. The recommendations which it finally submitted were called the Perrow Plan, or more idealistically the "freedom of choice" plan.

It was not a new approach to the desegregation problem except in details. The principle—that of removing the element of compulsion from attendance at integrated public schools, facilitating resort to segregated private schools and allowing each locality to solve its own problem—had been embodied in the Gray Commission recommendations in 1955. It had been expounded and urged persistently for two years past by Leon Dure, a farmer and retired journalist of Charlottesville. With eloquent emphasis upon the principle of "freedom of association," Dure had conducted a one-man campaign in "letters to the editor," pamphlets and newspaper advertisements. Dure's enthusiasm—though not the exact state of affairs in all respects —was to be reflected in his comment a year later that the plan "has transformed a Southern state from a chaos of closed schools and the agony of general despair into a situation of racial peace, well nigh total agreement and unheardof educational prosperity."

Following substantially the recommendations of the Perrow Commission, the legislature in a twenty-five-day session enacted both the local option provision (to take effect March 1, 1960) and a new tuition grant law. Under the latest tuition aid plan the grants were called "scholarships;" and they were made available to any children who might request them in attending non-sectarian private schools, without reference to segregation or integration. Other laws were passed calculated to aid the new private schools, including one to permit the sale of public school property upon approval by the voters of a locality in a referendum and one to permit localities to provide free transportation to pupils attending private schools.

The Virginia Committee for Public Schools now had a membership of over 22,000 and was still growing. William M. Lightsey of Arlington, one of the earliest leaders in the movement, had been engaged as its full-time executive secretary. Its officers and the members of its executive committee and its advisory committee formed an impressive list of prominent Virginians; and it was an ally now of the state administration. The Committee brought its influence effectively to bear in the events of February, March and April, supporting the recommendations of the Perrow Commission and opposing all anti-public school initiatives. Numerous statements were issued and analyses of proposed legislation were furnished to the members of the General Assembly. President Buck and Executive Secretary Lightsey, reinforced by representatives of eight local units, argued vigorously before legislative committees. The organization was to continue to combat recurring efforts to revive massive resistance throughout the year.

Governor Almond vigorously supported the Perrow Commission's recommendations, which had become the administration program. The administration forces also beat down attempts on the part of the "massive resistance bloc" to set in motion procedures to strike out the requirement that the state operate a public school system from the state constitution.

Though the opposition was tough and bitter now, the Governor still dominated the legislative session. The Byrd organization was clearly split at this point. Lieutenant-Governor A. E. S. Stephens and half a dozen able state Senators, Perrow, Edward L. Breeden, Earl Fitzpatrick, Charles R. Fenwick, Edward E. Willey and Harry C. Stuart—all with long organization background—supported Almond's policies and were to remain his staunch supporters. But the Governor was obliged to rely also on a motley group which included moderates, anti-Byrd liberals and several Republicans. As we have seen, the closely-knit "massive resistance bloc" came precariously close to having its way on the crucial issue of local option. On the other hand, there was evidence of greater support for the new policy among the people of the state than was reflected in the General Assembly.

At a number of points during this story of massive resistance we have had reason to suspect that Virginia's political leaders, instead of being hog-tied in constructive impulses by the prejudice of their constituents, were actually more extreme in their opposition to school desegregation than the people of the state as a whole. Such an attitude on the part of political leadership has been a not unusual phenomenon in the South during this period of turmoil over the segregation question.

If we ask why the politician is not inclined to cater to the more temperate elements of the electorate, the answer is not hard to find. Extremists are more effective politically than moderates in equal number. The former shout their views from the housetops. They vote in elections and bring others to the polls. Many of them abuse and intimidate their moderate neighbors. On the other hand, the silent moderate is likely only to cast his single furtive vote.

It is an unhappy circumstance also that the small rural counties are overrepresented in the legislature of every Southern state. These districts, with their disproportionate political power, are generally the areas of most intense race prejudice and fiercest hostility to school desegregation.

In Virginia the local option bill passed the state Senate by a vote of only twenty to nineteen. But more equitable representation in that body, it may be justly presumed, would have resulted in a much larger majority on the moderate side. Those who voted for local option represented 1,830,490 white constituents; those who voted against it represented 1,241,514. The Negro population of Virginia was more or less unanimously in favor of the local option approach.

The massive resisters made one more determined effort at the polls, in the form of a movement to "purge" the General Assembly of moderate members in the Democratic primary of July 14. The Defenders of State Sovereignty gave the signal, when it met in state convention May 23 and called on the voters to replace enough moderates with resisters to cancel the Almond-Perrow majority.

The results of the Democratic primary (which is generally tantamount to election in Virginia) made only a slight increase in moderate strength, but dealt what, in the circumstances, was a decisive rebuff to the massive resisters. The latter's main targets, state Senators Armistead L. Boothe, Blake T. Newton, Edward L. Breeden and Edward E. Haddock, were renominated by handsome margins.

To a degree unequalled during the previous four years, Virginia now turned its attention to matters other than race segregation. Distasteful in varying degrees, but tolerable to most, the state had found at least the germ of a solution of the vexing school problem. Developments on the segregation front began to receive smaller headlines, and the echoes of bitter controversy ceased to fill the daily press.

Governor Almond became an eloquent defender of public schools. He delivered three commencement addresses in June, 1959.

At Longwood College in crucial Prince Edward County, the Governor said that to abolish public education "would be to surrender to those whose purpose it is to destroy us. . . . Our freedom, our hopes, or aims, our very existence depend upon public education." At William and Mary College he said: "Public education has been the contributory factor in making Virginia the great state she is. . . . Public education must not be abandoned."

An address at the commencement exercises of the private school which had substituted all the year for the public high school in Warren County was probably Almond's most delicate assignment.

No error could be more grave [he said to the patrons of this private school]—no mistake more costly, than to succumb to the blandishments of those who would have Virginia abandon public education and thereby consign a generation of children to the darkness of illiteracy, the pits of indolence and dependency and the dungeons of delinquency.

The issues revolving around public education will confront the next session of the General Assembly. I have taken my stand. We must save, sustain and support the cause of public education in Virginia. I call upon all Virginians who believe in the soundness and righteousness of that position to rally to my support before it is too late. . . .

Actually, contrary to general expectations in the spring and summer, the question of public school segregation did not confront the General Assembly as a major issue when it met again in January, 1960.

At his Labor Day picnic in the apple orchards, Senator Byrd had broken a long silence on the subject to declare: "I stand now as I stood when I first urged massive resistance." But it sounded like a voice out of the past. By the end of the year all but a handful of fanatics in the legislature realized that monolithic massive resistance was dead.

The fight would go on. The extreme segregationists and the hard core of the Byrd machine had become a fiercely vindictive anti-Almond faction, and the battle lines were drawn. But the main fight would be waged on issues unrelated to school segregation.

The part which public interest, political expediency and personal feeling respectively play, or the degree to which the three are blended, in the motives of politicians is always an interesting speculation. Governor Almond in the autumn had announced his intention to request the legislature to enact a 3 per cent sales tax. Apart from the problem of the state's growing financial needs, it probably occurred to the Governor that a battle royal on a fiscal issue would be a wholesome distraction from the insidious and explosive segregation controversy.

On the other hand, the devotees of massive resistance undoubtedly had good reasons, related to the public welfare, for opposing the sales tax, which Virginia had been spared until now. It was an unpopular proposal. But one may be excused for suspecting that other considerations contributed to the zeal and near-unanimity with which the "massive resistance bloc" moved into action to defeat the Governor's initiative. The fight was bitter and tempers flared.

Almond was later to recover a hair's-breadth margin of control and secure the enactment of substantially the remainder of his program, including a dramatic increase in the budget, which the economy-minded Byrd faction strenuously opposed. But in the much-publicized sales tax fight, the Governor went down to inglorious defeat. The bill was killed in committee on February 18, and its chief executioners were Speaker Moore and State Senator Harry Byrd, Jr.

Almond was incensed. In a television appearance the next day, he referred to Moore and Byrd by name and proclaimed a political schism of possibly historic significance when he fumed: "If these gentlemen want to play it rough, that suits me, for the remainder of this administration and for the days to come after the close of this administration."

In thus declaring war upon Senator Byrd's comrade and chief spokesman and upon his son, Almond at last was openly defying the Senator himself.

Only one Governor of Virginia had ever done that before. James H. Price was the other governor (1938–1942) in whose candidacy Byrd had acquiesced only after it was apparent that he could not be beaten. Price was a handsome, friendly gentleman of extraordinary personal charm. Though his manner never descended from the traditional gentility which Virginians admire in their leaders, he attracted people in all walks of life. His political strength rested upon the sheer personal friendship of thousands of Virginians.

But Price's political outlook was liberal. When he displayed increasing enthusiasm for President Roosevelt and the New Deal, which were anathema to Byrd, the latter's initial tolerance turned into unrelenting hostility. The pro-Byrd majority in the legislature turned on the hapless Governor and obstructed or scuttled most of his program. When "Jim" Price's term expired, he found himself abandoned by most of his political friends and turned out to lonely pasture, while the

Byrd organization became more firmly entrenched than ever before. Price died two years later—many said, "of a broken heart."

When Almond broke with Byrd, the Price story came back to many of the older generation. Almond himself had known Price well, and he was mindful of Price's experience. But Almond is far from being another Jim Price, and Virginia of today is different from the Old Dominion of twenty years ago. It was often said of the courteous, sensitive Price that he was "too much a gentleman." Almond is essentially a fighter, one who knows all the tricks and likes to wrestle with no holds barred. Price was an ineffectual public speaker; Almond is a natural, irrepressible orator, unmatched in Virginia in his ability to sway crowds of people.

The population of Virginia has increased by over a million since the Price administration. Most of the newcomers are relatively liberal; they have the habit of voting on Election Day—which deplorably thousands of native Virginians have not—and they are by no means prepared to leave their politics to an apparatus like the Byrd machine. One fast-growing Congressional district, the Tenth, has seceded decisively from the Byrd political orbit. The rural counties, long the machine's chief source of power, have been lagging in population growth far behind the cities, where dissent flourishes. The Negro vote and the labor vote, both hostile to the Byrd machine, have been steadily increasing.

The machine was showing signs of senility and loss of its traditional magic before massive resistance to public school desegregation gave it a shot in the arm. Its candidates came alarmingly close to losing the gubernatorial elections of 1949 and 1953. A group of insurgent liberals, called the "Young Turks," fought the machine to a standstill in the legislature of 1954 on an issue of budget retrenchment.

The "Young Turks," without the nickname, are stirring again. Lindsay Almond's own future will depend in large measure on his ability to hold consistently henceforth to a course which he has, with supreme inconsistency, adopted, and to hold the support of the liberals, who hated him before but are grateful to him now for engineering the change. Other able leaders, whose moderate approach to the school problem during the whole trying period is a matter of consistent and heartbreaking record, are moving now with buoyant step and holding their heads high again.

It has often been said that nothing less than an issue of epoch-making importance could ever break the hold of the Byrd machine upon Virginia. Massive resistance to school desegregation at least met that specification. The Virginia tradition of oligarchic, "organization" rule is older than Harry Byrd's identification with politics, and it may outlive the Senator. It is the chief bulwark of the presently decimated Byrd machine, which has re-formed its ranks. But this hard core is not The Organization in the old omnipotent sense. It will have to fight perennially for survival against a manifestly powerful liberal opposition; it will have to take its turn at the normal political alternatives of ascendancy and coalition with the enemy or eclipse. Even of Virginia politics, it may be said at long last: "The old order changeth, yielding place to new."

We left Governor Almond before the television camera, dealing roughly with Harry Byrd, Jr., and Blackburn Moore. The same evening 1,200 Democrats gathered in a function which has come to have peculiar political significance in Virginia—the Jefferson-Jackson Day dinner. Outside of a dozen Republican counties, and excepting a rare Republican leader like Dalton, the legislators, mayors, sheriffs, party chairmen, etc. who assemble at this annual event form the political confraternity which runs the state.

On a platform at one end of the long dining room at the Hotel John Marshall sit the black-tied dignitaries: the guest speaker, U.S. senators and congressmen and the Governor, Lieutenant-Governor and Attorney General of Virginia. Before the speaker is presented, each of the Virginia dignitaries is introduced, and the brief applause which follows is carefully watched for its political significance. The duration of the applause for each was recorded with precision this year by the *Richmond Times-Dispatch*.

Harry Byrd, Sr., was unable to be present, but eight minutes of applause greeted a mention of that name. Congressman and former Governor Tuck, the fire-eating resister ("If they won't go along with us, I say make 'em!") led all but the Governor with eleven seconds of applause. The Lieutenant-Governor and the Attorney General receive ten and nine seconds of applause respectively. Friends of Speaker Moore, whom Almond had attacked earlier in the day, might have been expected to show their sympathy with pointed applause for him, but Moore was applauded for only five seconds. Governor Almond received eighteen seconds of lusty applause.

Two other names were also mentioned jointly—Thomas Jefferson and Andrew Jackson. They were applauded for two seconds.

The congeniality of this gathering is remarkable. The milk of human kindness flows through the long dining room and out into the lobby, where Virginia Democrats greet old friends, slap backs and laugh together for hours before and after dinner. Most of the politicians whom we have met on this pilgrimage through Virginia's massive resistance were there. Nor is "harmony" at the Jefferson-Jackson Day dinner all a matter of expediency. Tonight a remarkable substratum of genuine friendship shows through the political animosities of yesterday—and tomorrow. At this festive gathering, these men who argue and orate and intrigue and quarrel over the problems of the commonwealth are comrades and Virginia gentlemen. And there we take leave of them.

32. A CORNER TURNED

VIRGINIA's massive resistance collapsed in the spring of 1959, five years after the Supreme Court decision. At that time public school segregation was nearing an end in a vast "border" area between the North and the South in the United States. But adjustment to the ruling in the former Confederate states, where Negroes were far more numerous, still had a long, painful road to travel. In South Carolina, Georgia, Florida, Alabama, Louisiana and Mississippi not a single breach had been made in the wall of race segregation in public schools. Recalcitrance, resistance and defiance in various forms still described the prevailing attitude toward the high court's ruling in most of the South.

Nevertheless, a certain corner had been turned. The deliberate adventure of "massive resistance," which proponents of the Southern Manifesto had envisioned as a dramatic all-Southern challenge of the validity of the Supreme Court decision, had run its course. The issue had been joined in what was the foremost bastion of the old Southern Confederacy, and federal authority had prevailed.

Virginia had embraced massive resistance as an official state policy. It had resurrected the ancient doctrine of interposition to give it historic solemnity and a fatuous claim to legality.

And the South had looked to Virginia more than to any other state for leadership in this crisis. Virginia, with its glorious role in the early history of the republic and again in the struggle for the great Lost Cause—also with its genteel and honored political leadership of today—was surely indicated to carry the banner of the South in this latest conflict.

Virginia's posture had dignified and encouraged resistance to the desegregation rulings in all her sister Southern states. The mental processes of Governor Orval Faubus are difficult to fathom, but there are many in his state of Arkansas who believe that the events leading to the tragic convulsions of Little Rock would not have occurred had it not been for the example of apparent defiance of federal authority set by the conservative and respected leaders of the Old Dominion.

The debacle of massive resistance in Virginia, therefore, had a profound effect elsewhere in the South. Neither bravado nor chicanery, nor legislative stratagems, nor the Southern loyalties of Virginia-born jurists had caused federal courts to swerve from faithful pronouncement of the law of the land in the face of this challenge. Outright disobedience of federal court orders, armed rebellion—these courses had never been seriously contemplated by responsible Virginians. Elsewhere in the South, such fantasies were mortally bludgeoned by the dispatch of the 101st Airborne to Little Rock in 1957. They were all but extinguished by the cold facts of the Virginia story. The substitution of private schools for public schools as a means of evading racial integration—though this lesson would sink in more slowly—had proven egregiously impracticable. The truth came quietly home to many Southern politicians that "you can't win" against the Supreme Court and the government of the United States.

This writer entered the service, in March, 1959, of the Southern Regional Council, an organization of Southerners dedicated to the elimination of race discrimination. My work brought me into contact with politicians, editors and other leaders in many sections of the South. I found intense interest in the developments in Virginia, much more than was reflected in published comments. Politicians were deeply impressed.

In Georgia, where moderation had become anathema and a fiercely segregationist state administration stood determined to close public schools when desegregation orders should take effect, former Governor Ellis Arnall announced that he was opposed to the closing of schools to escape integration. Before the year was over a number of Georgia politicians were to take a similar stand.

In Florida the year had opened with dark forebodings. Segregationist leaders were drafting a pile of "anti-integration" bills which would outdo Virginia's ill-fated massive resistance legislation. There were no less than thirty-two such bills when the legislature met on April 1. Legislators of the dominant group were said to be ready to vote for "any anti-integration bill they could get their hands on." A "runaway" session was predicted. But in the meantime the Virginia resistance structure had collapsed. Thanks to that lesson, and the skillful leadership of Governor LeRoy Collins, Florida was spared the massive resistance ordeal. The school-closing bills and other extremist proposals fell by the wayside. Token public school integration began in Miami the following September, without disorder, rescuing Florida from the list of totally recalcitrant states.

Long-suffering moderates everywhere in the South took heart. "Save-the-public-schools" movements gathered strength in Arkansas, Georgia and Louisiana. Information was eagerly sought on the manner in which citizens had worked effectively under this banner in Virginia. In Little Rock business leaders began to assert themselves, conscious of the economic penalties of racial turmoil. The Women's Emergency Committee to Open Our Schools moved into dynamic action, with over 1,000 members. In fact, moderate elements at last came into the ascendancy in that troubled city, when the extremist members of the Little Rock board of education were replaced by moderates in a popular election.

I talked with Governor Faubus in June, in the faint hope that he might be influenced by the course which Governor Almond of Virginia had followed. Federal court decisions at this point had placed Faubus in a somewhat similar situation. The Arkansas Governor's reaction to my approach was entirely negative, but it was evident nonetheless that Virginia's abandonment of massive resistance had given him food for thought. Integration began in Little Rock public schools the following September—without the presence of soldiers—and this time the Governor offered no interference.

In September and October, 1960, in each of the states where a beginning had been made, public school desegregation was extended. The gain was still small—fourteen additional school districts in the eleven-state region—but for the first time since 1954 the adjustments were made in an atmosphere of complete tranquillity and order.

The nation was shocked and revolted, however, by the convulsions which ensued from the court-ordered admission on November 14 of four Negro children to two previously all-white schools in New Orleans. It is not pertinent here to dwell on that dismaying episode beyond observing that we have had no more tragic example of the interference of politicians and a state administration in the process of desegregation under federal court order. In New Orleans the city authorities, the school board and a clear majority of the public were prepared, albeit reluctantly, to accept this small step toward desegregation in an orderly manner. But the Governor of Louisiana and the state legislature not only resorted to every conceivable governmental trick to prevent execution of the federal court order, but actually stimulated public hostility and turmoil. The legislature's response to New Orleans rioting was a joint resolution commending "the parents who withdrew their children from the schools . . . for their courageous stand against the forces of integration. . . ."

In the foregoing story of the massive resistance era in Virginia, I have dwelt extensively on the political manifestations. The South's problem, of course, is broader and deeper than politics. Ancient custom and prejudice, sedulous racist propaganda, widespread dissemination of misinformation and the strange, irrational contagion of race hatred are basic ingredients. The path toward solution is crowded with difficulties, both real and imagined, outside of the political realm; and the imagined difficulties have become in effect real difficulties—the greatest difficulties. These depressing phenomena have been voluminously and ably discussed by other writers. The political factor has received less analytical attention.

Theoretically, once the Supreme Court had spoken, compliance with its ruling was one for the conscience of individuals or a matter between federal courts and school administrators. Actually, and in a negative sense, it has become the main business of politicians. The political incubus hangs heavily now over the whole problem. It is through breaks in the political clouds that we must look for a change in the tone of public utterances, for the restoration of free discussion and for measures to make possible those beginnings of school integration in practice which cause imagined difficulties to disappear.

Disappointment is sometimes expressed because no Southern leader on a high pedestal has called boldly for an end to flouting of the law and an end to the shame of race discrimination. That kind of miracle is not to be expected. The politician anywhere is helpless unless he holds office or has a following; and in most of the South today a politician who advocated school integration out of hand would soon have neither. Nevertheless, a constructive attitude, short of that, on the part of Virginia's leaders in the relatively propitious atmosphere of 1954–1955 might have changed the course of Southern history. Generally speaking, the politicians of the South have failed dismally to meet their responsibilities of leadership in this crisis. Their activities on the whole have tended to unprepare, rather than to prepare, the public for the inevitable social change. No small part of the blame for the confusion and hysteria and the public disorder must be laid at their door.

But the men of conscience in Southern politics, who are far more numerous than many suppose, face a real and painful problem. It is much more difficult in most of the South than it was intrinsically in Virginia—or in Arkansas. Southern politicians have suffered great inner travail during the past six years. I have talked with many of them, with some intimately. "I try to lead my people," one anguished legislator said to me. "I try to lead my people, but how can I lead them if I get too far out in front?" Some Southern leaders have gotten far out in front —and survived. Governor LeRoy Collins of Florida and William B. Hartsfield, Atlanta's indomitable Mayor, are heartening examples.

The Virginia story is a boon to those leaders of the South who, convinced either of the wrongness of race segregation or of the necessity of upholding the nation's supreme law, would like to get on with the imperative task of adjustment. What happened in Virginia sharpened the alternatives; it resolved the issue pragmatically into one of desegregation as ordered by federal courts or the closing of schools. The dreadful alternative of abandoning public education is now the single desperate road of defiance. In the last analysis even the Deep South will not go down that road.

As this choice is increasingly recognized, a path emerges, leading on solid ground out of the morass. The South is not ready to listen to an assault upon prejudice from its political leaders, but men of good will can rally to this cause with a minimum of odium or political peril. They can fight to preserve public schools on the only terms on which public schools can be preserved. Idealists would like to raise a nobler standard, but in the present frame of reference that is enough. On that platform, and moving on from it in time, enlightened political leadership can surmount this hurdle and clear the path of advance to the South's great destiny.

INDEX